We are *ALL*

Innocent

by Reason of

Insanity

We Are

ALL

Innocent

by Reason of

Insanity

The Mechanics of Compassion

by Kathleen Brugger

For Arthur,

who is at the center of everything I do

Table of Contents

Part 3: Love is Sanity

Preface

This book is the fruit of a long-term collaboration with my husband Arthur Hancock. In the more than thirty years of our relationship we have been looking for answers to questions such as: what is the meaning of life?, why do we suffer?, who are we?

In our first book, *The Game of God*, which we co-authored (cartoons by Arthur), we presented our answer to the question, "Why does the universe exist?" Oprah called this "a great book about God." Tim Allen included it in his recommended reading list at the end of his bestseller, *I'm Not Really Here*.

Then Arthur and I turned our attention to the human condition. Why are happiness and peace so elusive? Why is love so rare? Our philosophy of universal human insanity was developed through years of observation of ourselves and humanity at large. *We Are ALL Innocent by Reason of Insanity* is an exposition of this philosophy, and Arthur's forthcoming memoir, *Exposing Myself*, uses his life story to illustrate the theory.

Recently I gave the following quick synopsis to a new acquaintance: "Most of us think we perceive reality directly and accurately. But we don't. What we see is an individual mind-generated reality, heavily distorted by our beliefs and assumptions. We confuse our subjective opinions with objective facts. We're all deluded about what is real, and this is why we're all insane."

I could see that he found this a dubious proposition, and I was pretty sure it was because he was convinced that he did perceive reality directly and accurately.

The analogy of a 3D movie may help to illustrate the concept of universal insanity. When a 3D movie is being made, two cameras film simultaneously from slightly separated positions. The final film superimposes the offset perspectives. When you wear polarizing glasses those two images are separated and delivered to the appropriate eye, and you perceive the illusion of three-dimensions on a flat movie screen. But when you look at the film without glasses, it's blurry, as if it's out of focus. If you watch too long it's disorientating and nauseating.

Humans are the product of over three billion years of evolution on this planet. An organism survives when its subjective reality (however rudimentary) is closely aligned to objective physical reality. For example, if we weren't able to distinguish the crouching tiger from the obscuring foliage we'd be dead. Our ability to construct an accurate model of physical reality in our minds is quite remarkable.

But there is another reality in our minds, a subjective reality, and this doesn't match physical, objective reality. It is offset from objective reality by a small amount, depending upon the content of our personal subjective beliefs. This offset causes dissonance in our minds, analogous to the way the 3D picture causes nausea. This dissonance is our delusional insanity, and the more our subjective reality is offset from objective reality, the more insane we are.

As 3D films show, it doesn't take much offset to create an uncomfortable distortion. This is why it can be hard for us "normal" people to grasp our insanity, because our everyday actions appear to prove that we are in touch with objective reality. We can navigate our cars through rush hour traffic, handle the demands of our job, shop for groceries, cook dinner, bathe the kids—all this seems to indicate that we are accurately perceiving objective reality. But accompanying these actions are the distortions caused by our subjective reality: we're unhappy, or anxious, or depressed, or wish we could be doing something else.

We have all been programmed to think this internal dissonance is completely normal. It's "normal" if by that word you mean what people live with every day. It's also "normal" in the sense of being an evolutionary inevitability. But this dissonance is exactly what I mean by universal insanity. We all confuse our subjective reality with objective reality, and when life doesn't go according to our subjective-reality-script, we feel anger, anxiety, or depression.

Recognizing my insanity means I stop confusing my subjective beliefs with objective reality. It doesn't mean I don't have a subjective point-of-view, it means I eliminate a lot of the dissonance—conflicts, disappointments, problems—in my life.

Asheville NC
May 2013

Part One

We Are All Insane

When we remember we are all mad,
the mysteries disappear and life stands explained.
- Mark Twain[1]

1

Virtual Reality

Thomas Jefferson is revered in the United States, in part for his inspiring language in the Declaration of Independence: "We hold these truths to be self-evident, that all men are created equal, that they are endowed by their Creator with certain unalienable rights, that among these are life, liberty, and the pursuit of happiness."

Noble words, but ones that reveal an astonishing cognitive dissonance in the mind of the man who wrote them. Thomas Jefferson owned slaves. Clearly he could believe in the ideal of liberty and equality for "all men," yet simultaneously believe that *some* men could be enslaved and treated unequally because of their skin color.

Today we congratulate ourselves that we're beyond this kind of confused thinking on race, but most of us still believe in the concept of race itself. We think there really are "Caucasian" and "Asian" and "Black" humans. But, according to scientists, including the majority of anthropologists, the concept of race exists entirely in our minds; there is only *one* race, the human race.[2]

What would it mean if racial categories were just an invention of the human mind, if the "fact" of race turns out to be an illusory mind-generated reality?

A friend of mine shaved off *half* his moustache one morning, and then walked around all day enjoying people's reactions. He couldn't believe how long it took most people to become aware of his half-moustache.

People "saw" him with his moustache intact—entirely missing the reality that half of it was gone. When they finally noticed the half-moustache their faces always registered shock (realizing how out of touch with reality they were) before dissolving into laughter.

When I was a teenager my favorite book was *The Heart is a Lonely Hunter*, by Carson McCullers.[3] Not long after I met Arthur, my husband of over thirty years, I went to his apartment and this was one of three books on his desk. But I was surprised when I heard him talk about it, because it sounded like he was describing a completely different book. In my mind it was the story of a young girl whose dreams of a creative life were squashed by economic realities. In Arthur's mind it was the story of a deaf-mute and the people who found in him an outlet to express their frustrations and dreams. One book, but two very separate realities.

Think of the most basic element of any argument: "You're wrong," "No, *you're* wrong." From a couple arguing about who forgot to mail the rent check to two nations fighting a war over a disputed boundary, disagreements arise from separate realities in the minds of the participants.

Most of us think we perceive reality directly and accurately. That is not true. We all live in our own individual, mind-generated reality.

The idea that we see only a mind-generated reality feels wrong; the sensation that we experience the physical world directly and perceive it accurately is very strong. For example, when I want to pick my shoe up off the floor I can accurately locate the physical object—the shoe is here on the floor, not over there on the dining table—and I can precisely move my hand to its location and pick it up. Surely this means I'm experiencing the physical world the way it is!

The disquieting truth is I'm not.

Just for starters, we have blind spots in both of our eyes. In the middle of the retina, where the optical nerve attaches, there are no light receptor cells. We literally cannot see part of the visual field before us. Yet our mental image of reality does not match what our eyes actually see; the picture in our mind doesn't include large black holes in the center. Our minds fill in the blanks with what they think *should* be there, built from our expectations of reality, the information surrounding the blind spot, and our experience of how the world works.

Optical illusions are amusing and shocking because they let us see that we do not perceive reality accurately.

For example, in the illustration below the center bar is the same shade of grey all the way across, yet our perception is that it's lighter on the right.

When I was a child I loved to count the time between a flash of lightning and the sound of thunder—every five seconds of separation meant a mile. But I never stopped to consider what that meant about other perceptions of light and sound. When a friend calls to me from across the street, I perceive that his mouth moves and the sound comes out of his mouth simultaneously. But just like the lightning's sound coming slower than the flash, my friend's voice doesn't hit my ears until after my eyes see his mouth move.

Not only do visual and aural signals travel to our eyes and ears at different rates, our brain processes the two perceptions at different rates. And somehow our brain still links them together as one and the same event.[4]

Ventriloquists exploit our brain's processing to trick us into believing that their voice is coming out of their puppet's mouth. I love Triumph the Insult Comic Dog by Robert Smigel. Triumph is a crude rubber dog, and it's absurdly obvious that "his" voice is coming from off-screen, yet the illusion is created that Triumph is really speaking or singing.[5]

The art of foley is another example of how our brain's processing of visual and aural cues can create an illusion of reality. We see someone's leg breaking and we hear celery snapping, we see someone being punched and we hear a raw steak being hit, we see someone riding a horse and hear two coconut halves banging together (see Monty Python's *The Holy Grail* for an amusing riff on this illusion[6]), and we really believe we're hearing the actual sound of whatever action we're seeing. I've thought about this while watching action movies—how does anyone know what the sound of a fifty-foot monster kicking around buses on a city street sounds like?

Clearly there is some mental processing going on that interprets perceptual information *before* it gets to our awareness.

We have to learn to see and hear. As infants we learn how to process sensory information to create a mental picture of reality in our brain. We are taught first by our parents and then by everyone around us how to interpret the input of our senses.

We look with our eyes but see with our brains.

A friend of mine described how, for most of his life, he had never paid much attention to pregnant women. But when he learned he was going to become a father, "Suddenly large numbers of pregnant women started popping out of the landscape. I found myself noticing them and observing them with intense interest. After the birth of my daughter this legion of pregnant females receded back into the mists of my indifference."

Of course there weren't more pregnant women than normal; it was just because of his personal interest that he saw them. And they didn't suddenly disappear after the birth of his daughter; he was just no longer paying attention to pregnant women and so from his point-of-view they ceased to exist.

Our brains take the sensory stimuli generated by actual reality (whatever that may be) and create virtual models in our minds. We see only the mental representation of a thing, not the thing itself.

This means we all live in our own individual virtual reality. We do not see actual reality; we see our mind-generated virtual reality projected on an internal screen of awareness.

Our mind-generated reality is more than just a model of physical reality; it includes abstract, subjective perceptions also.

Psychology textbooks are filled with long lists of common errors in our subjective perception of reality. For example, there's the famous "Lake Wobegon effect": most people think they're above average (a statistical impossibility). There's wishful thinking: "One day I'll hit the lottery and all my problems will be solved." Denial: "I'm not an alcoholic—I just like to drink every night, and I've been doing it all my life without any problem." Or, "I'm not in an unhappy marriage—we never fight!" (Because we never talk to each other...) Rationalization: "It's okay that I steal paperclips from work because they'll never miss them."

These thinking errors can all be summed up in this line from the song "The Boxer" by Paul Simon: "A man hears what he wants to hear and disregards the rest."[7]

Our mind-generated virtual reality is a construct built of preconceptions, beliefs, and assumptions that cause us to see our world and ourselves in a rigid and unchanging way. We are boxed in by our beliefs about reality.

Someone (the source is disputed) said, "We do not see things as they are. We see things as we are."

Comedians make us laugh because they break open our individual reality-box: they challenge our fixed beliefs and force us to see life from an alternative point-of-view. They literally crack us up!

We like puns because they expose how our minds make assumptions based on the meaning of words. When it's revealed that our assumption of a word's meaning was incorrect, it turns our understanding of the joke upside down. Groucho Marx provides a great example: "Time flies like an arrow. Fruit flies like a banana."

❖

I knew an elderly woman named Bessie who was constantly harassed by an annoying entity named Whitney. Sometimes Whitney would sit on the end of Bessie's nose and try to take food off her spoon while she was eating. Whitney was always telling Bessie to "go get in the bed." While Whitney was invisible to everyone else, he was all too real to Bessie. Doctors would have diagnosed Bessie as delusional: seeing something not subject to objective confirmation by others.

Who hasn't experienced "seeing something not subject to objective confirmation by others" when they look in the mirror! How many readers can relate to this scenario: I'm oblivious to the weight I've gained when I gaze at my image in the mirror, seeing instead the thinner self of years past. Then I put on a pair of pants I haven't worn for a while and feel surprise when they're tight.

Webster's New Universal, Unabridged Dictionary defines "delusion" as: *a fixed, false belief that is resistant to reason or confrontation with actual fact.*

Once I gained some weight and a favorite skirt was so tight I moved the buttons so it would fit better. Believe it or not, at the time I was actually convinced that something about the *skirt* had changed.

I was completely unwilling to admit the obvious fact that I had gained weight. I was resistant to reason or confrontation with actual fact. I was delusional.

A white man of my acquaintance, who I'll call Bob, once suffered a diabetic coma. An ambulance was called to his home. Though unconscious, Bob was able to hear the EMS personnel talking. The white members of the team were repeatedly ready to give up on him, but the sole black technician refused and kept working until he brought Bob back to life. When describing this scene later, Bob, a life-long racist, would refer to this valiant man as "the nigger": "I could hear them talking and one would say, 'He's gone, let's stop,' but the nigger would say, 'No, let's keep working on him.'" Even the objective reality of a man saving his life was not enough to shake Bob's fixed reality that a black man is a "nigger."

Psychologists tell us that we build models of reality in our minds, and we use these models to navigate the world. We do not see actual reality, whatever that might be. We see only a mind-generated model of reality. No matter how good a model it may be, it is still just a system of beliefs about reality.

When we believe our mind-generated model of reality is actual reality we are delusional.

Delusional is just another word for insane.

What better explanation for the human condition than delusional insanity? What better way to explain why loneliness, fear, and hatred are so familiar and love so rare? Why bigotry and prejudice are still so common? Why peace and cooperation elude us? Why so many people need to use alcohol and drugs just to get through another day, seeking a satisfaction not available in sobriety? Why more than one in ten Americans take anti-depressants just so they can function? Why billions of human beings live in desperate poverty and ignorance while a tiny few live lives of wasteful luxury and self-indulgence? Why the human race totters on the brink of the supreme folly of self-extinction, via environmental collapse or thermonuclear disaster?

Of course there are other explanations for this list of human ills. Judeo-Christian theology, a world-view that has exerted tremendous influence on western culture, says that humans are cursed with something called "original sin" and are, therefore, inherently evil;

God gave humans free will and we choose evil because we *are* evil.

One of Gary Larson's *Far Side* cartoons shows a plump young man stretched out on a psychiatrist's couch, his mouth gaping wide in self-absorbed monologue, while the bearded shrink is quietly writing on his pad, "Just plain <u>nuts</u>."[8]

Which is the better explanation for the chronic human ills listed above: "humans are just plain <u>nuts</u>"—evolving apes understandably confused about the nature of reality and necessarily making mistakes out of their confusion and ignorance; or "humans are just plain <u>evil</u>"—stubborn wicked creatures who sadistically (or masochistically) use their free will to *choose* pain, suffering, and wrongdoing when they know better? Which explanation offers us hope for a different future? If we are just plain nuts then we have some hope of finding sanity. If we are just plain evil what is there to do? How does one overcome intrinsic evil?

If universal human insanity is the cause of the human condition, we can immediately begin to envision the possibility of a cure; we can begin to imagine the possibilities for humankind when we are liberated from our delusions. Imagine realizing that all our crimes and misdemeanors, our mistakes, and our embarrassing blunders are simply products of our delusional thinking and not willful wrongdoing! Imagine realizing that punishing ourselves and others for wrongdoing is literally as absurd (and counterproductive) as punishing the inmates of a lunatic asylum for misbehaving.

At first blush the idea that we're insane sounds like a horrible thing, but actually there's great news here. Realizing our insanity can empower us by freeing us from the delusion that we're in control. Because we're insane we can't be blamed and shamed for all those misdeeds and wrongs that haunt us—we're innocent by reason of insanity.

In addition, when we realize that everyone is insane, we have the key to compassion. We understand why people (including ourselves) do mean or hurtful things: we know not what we do.

Being innocent by reason of insanity is in no way a blank check or license to kill. It doesn't mean it's okay to do mean and hurtful things; it means we understand that those actions are motivated by insanity, not willful choice. We will still put people in prison if we can't figure out any other way to prevent them from hurting others.

But we will think differently about who they are: they're not evil monsters, they're sick.

Innocent has two meanings. The first is "not guilty." Most of us believe that we *are* guilty—by reason of sanity. Happily, as we shall see, this is not the truth. When we recognize our insanity we realize that we are *innocent* of all the charges we have levied against ourselves.

The other meaning of innocent is "virtuous, flawless, without sin or moral wrong." By realizing our insanity, we can experience this meaning of innocent, analogous to the innocence of a child.

After spending a lifetime convinced that we're sane, the idea that we're all insane is guaranteed to meet with some resistance. I know from experience how difficult facing this truth is, but I also know how liberating it can be.

Not only is insanity universal; there is absolutely nothing wrong with it: the universe is unfolding perfectly and without flaw. The pageant of evolution must include the epoch of insanity.

Evolving apes endowed with analytical thought are bound to go bananas...before they work the problem out.

2

Collective Reality

Western philosophers have been arguing about the nature of reality for hundreds of years: is there an actual reality out there or does it exist only in our minds? The 18th Century philosopher George Berkeley asserted that reality exists entirely in the mind. Dr. Samuel Johnson, hearing of this, indignantly exclaimed, "I refute it thusly!" and kicked his foot against a stone.

In this book I will assert that Berkeley and Johnson were both right. There is an actual reality out there *and* everyone has a unique perception of this reality in his or her mind. As we will see, all of us live in our own individual subjective reality.

In addition, every society develops a "consensus reality," a collective mind-generated reality. Our individual realities are constructed within the collective reality of our culture.

One of the reasons it's so hard to realize that we are living in a mind-generated reality is because when we conform to our culture's collective reality there is a lot of agreement that this reality is really real. It's often hard to even recognize the beliefs that underlie the collective reality of our own culture. Looking back in time helps, because collective cultural beliefs change.

For example, a few hundred years ago people of African descent weren't considered human by many Europeans and Americans. Africans were bought and sold in slavery because of a belief that these dark-skinned people were more like animals than humans. In a painfully slow process Western culture has changed its beliefs to recognize that all people, no matter the color of their skin, are equally human. But even today there is clear evidence that not everyone's reality has changed—there are still people in our culture whose reality includes the belief that a person with dark skin is inferior to a person with light skin.

Our cultural beliefs about the morality of exposed flesh are another example. In one of my earliest memories I'm running down the street in front of my house, and I'm only wearing shorts. I'm thinking, "Soon I'm going to be too old to do this, I'll have to wear a shirt." I grew up in Missouri where it gets very hot in the summer. Every year, from the age of five until puberty, I burned with anger in addition to the heat at being required to wear a shirt when my chest looked no different than my brother's. Why was he allowed to go topless and be cool, when it was "dirty" for childishly flat-chested me?

Even today I look at photos of young girls in bikinis, with those silly tops flapping over non-existent breasts, and feel the old anger at our primitive, prurient, and puritanical attitudes towards the human body. We could easily go on and question our culture's ridiculous ban on bare-breasted women of any age. *National Geographic* was the pornography of the pre-*Playboy* years and even better because you could appear to be improving your mind while feasting your eyes on the topless women of "backward" cultures that didn't share our obsession with hiding women's breasts.

Modern bikinis are so tiny they leave almost nothing to the imagination, but the absence of those pieces of fabric, covering three objectionable points of the female anatomy, would constitute indecent exposure in current American reality. Reality is different in much of Europe where topless beaches are normal; only one piece is required. Of course that one piece is still very important for both woman *and* men.

While the steadily increasing acceptance of nudity continues in the West, the conservative Islamic world still insists that women must be hidden; that exposed female flesh is immoral. Special bathing suits are available for Islamic women that look like skirted wetsuits with hoods. A typical suit has multiple pieces: a long-sleeved dress that ends above the knee, long pants to the ankle, and a head covering.

Homosexuality provides another example of changing cultural norms. Until 1973 the psychiatric community officially labeled homosexuality a mental illness—it was classified in the Diagnostic and Statistical Manual of Mental Disorders as a sexual deviation. In the last 40 years the change in our consensus reality has been swift; it won't be long until gay marriage is a completely accepted part of American culture.

Travel allows us to see that our culture's reality isn't the only way to view the world, and the dissonance caused by the clash of beliefs and assumptions has a name: culture shock. The reason we feel shock is because we take our culture's collective reality so for granted that we think it is actual reality. It's unsettling to experience an alternate reality.

We often use the word "myth" dismissively, as something just made-up, but this is exactly what our collective mind-generated reality is: something made-up, invented, to explain the mystery of existence to ourselves in order to make sense of it. Myth is a culture's collective mind-generated reality, how it describes the world.

For thousands of years humans told variations of the same story: gods lived and moved among us and ruled humanity and nature. The world was like a large hall. The earth was the floor and the sun, moon, and stars moved around the ceiling. We now see this as a primitive misconception of reality, but these gods and this world were very real to the people of that time.

Then Christianity took hold in the West. Christian cultures told a new story: up above the clouds was a place called Heaven and down below the ground was a place called Hell. These places were very real to people of the last millennia.

Now most of us look to science to define reality. Today we believe that the universe began in a Big Bang. This is our collective reality. And we think we are more in touch with reality than those earlier peoples who believed in Zeus or the fiery pits of Hell. We portray earlier cultures' mind-generated realities as quaint misconceptions based on limited understanding—the stars are holes in the ceiling—but we assume that our current mind-generated reality is authentic because it's based on science.

But science has continuously changed its description of the universe. One hundred years ago astronomers told us that what we saw in the night sky, a few thousand stars, was the entire universe.[9] Now we are told that what we see up there is just a very small portion of something called a galaxy, containing a hundred billion stars, one among hundreds of billions of galaxies in a mind-bogglingly large universe. And the latest news from physics is that our universe may be only one of an infinite number of multiverses.

You can be sure that in the future another society will look back with amusement upon our quaint myths, our primitive scientific explanations of the universe.

Collective realities are language-based. Long ago humans developed a level of language skill sophisticated enough to permit us to label and categorize things. As time passed we forgot that the labels were just convenient tools. We came to believe that they had separate, real existence.

For example, we divided the Earth into countries and have so completely forgotten that the divisions are arbitrary that we have fought endless battles over the invented boundaries. When people first saw the photos of our planet taken by Apollo astronauts in the 1960s it was a revelation—all those arbitrary borders are irrelevant when you comprehend the vastness of the blackness surrounding our precious globe of life.

We confuse the naming of a phenomenon with the understanding of it. We give a child a name and by the time that child has grown up she believes that name defines who she is. I was given the name "Kathleen" when I was born, but the only time I heard that name was when my mother was mad at me. I was known as "Kathy" during my childhood. But that name sounded square and boring to me, so when I graduated from college and moved to San Francisco I decided I should change my name to better suit the person I wanted to be. I became "Katie," because I believed "Katie" is the name of someone who is fun and adventurous.

A consensus reality is essential for a society to function; members must agree to agree about certain aspects of reality. Most of the members of our culture agree to stop at a red light, for instance. We learn as an infant that red means stop and green means go—and yellow means go very fast. There is nothing inherent in the color green that means "go," but it is useful to have that shared interpretation.

In his masterpiece *Up from Eden*, Ken Wilber quotes Don Juan, the Yaqui Indian shaman, describing to his student Carlos Castaneda (from the book *Journey to Ixtlan*) how we are all indoctrinated into the belief system of our culture:

Everyone who comes into contact with a child is a teacher who incessantly describes the world to him, until the moment when the child is capable of perceiving the world as it is described...We have no memory of that portentous moment, simply because none of us could possibly have had any point of reference to compare it to anything else...Reality, or the world we all know, is only a description..., an endless flow of perceptual interpretations which we, the individuals who share a specific membership, have learned to make in common.[10]

Mr. Wilber concludes, "This large, unconscious background of membership cognition, basically *linguistic* in nature, of shared sentiments, shared descriptive realities, and shared perceptions, alone can serve as the psychological support of a coherent society."[10]

Just because a group of people agree to believe in a collective reality does not make it real. It may make for a functioning society but it remains a collection of beliefs about actual reality. It is still a virtual, mind-generated reality.

❖

A random list of some of our culture's collective beliefs:

"Men are superior to women"—sexism is still rampant in American culture.

"God exists, and has a gender," and what a surprise, most people think God is male.

"Marriage is between two individuals." We're almost past "marriage is between a man and a woman" but we're a long way from accepting anything but monogamy.

"Fat is ugly." This is not true in other cultures or times. In some countries in Africa obesity is actually revered; in Renaissance art, plump females were considered aesthetically pleasing, as epitomized in the paintings of Rubens.[11]

"It is not okay for women to have hair on the face, under the arms, or on the legs. However, it is okay for men to have hair in these regions."

"Men do not wear skirts." The Scottish kilt is the obvious

example of a different cultural belief on this subject; many tourists are shocked on their first visit to Fiji to see large powerful male policemen in a uniform that includes a skirt, called a "sulu."

"Sex is dirty. Explicit sex in movies is obscene, but extreme violence is okay, even for children."

"Humans are separate from nature."

"Private property is sacred; it's okay to kill someone who threatens your property."

"Black is the color of mourning." In other cultures the color of mourning is white, purple, or red.

"I have an immortal soul that enters my body at (a) birth (b) conception (c) some other time...and leaves at death and goes (a) to heaven (b) to hell or (c) to some spiritual nirvana."

Examine your reaction to this list. Did you accept some as self-evident, true, and beyond question? That is, you believe they represent actual reality and not a consensual reality based on cultural beliefs?

Another example of cultural mind-generated reality is the price of art. What could justify a price of $11 million for a single painting of a Campbell soup can by Andy Warhol? When the artist created the original series of 32 soup-can paintings in 1962 only a handful of people were willing to pay $100 for a canvas, and over the years he painted hundreds more in the series. The only possible explanation for the price, paid at an art auction in 2006, is that a group of people agreed among themselves that a canvas painted by this artist has a high value.

Price bubbles are another example of consensual reality in action. Bubbles happen when people agree that a commodity is valuable and their belief pushes the price of that commodity up until it has no relation to any actual utilitarian value. The Dutch tulip bubble of the 1630s is a classic example.[12]

The housing bubble in the United States is a more recent example. In 2000, someone we know bought an ocean-view condo in Florida for $125,000. Five years later they sold that apartment for $415,000. In 2011, that very same condo was worth $180,000. Same condo, same view, same building. The only difference: the subjective perception of its value created by a housing mania that had seized our culture. The blatantly delusional belief, "housing prices will keep going up forever," had become part of millions of people's mind-generated reality, including that of economists who should have known better. Prices just reflected the delusion.

Soldiers in war must struggle with the cognitive dissonance created by the sudden permission to break one of society's most basic rules. Most cultures' consensual reality says it's necessary, even heroic, to kill within a war zone, but if you kill outside that zone you've committed murder and should be punished. Many books and films have focused on the psychological cost of this dissonance. In Monty Python's *The Meaning of Life*, a dying British soldier says to a passing officer:

> Better than staying at home, eh sir? At home if you kill someone they arrest you. Here they give you a gun, and show you what to do, sir. I mean, I killed fifteen of those buggers sir! Now at home they'd hang me. Here they give me a fucking medal sir![13]

As long as our thoughts and behaviors conform to our culture's collective mind-generated reality we are accepted as normal and sane. Any deviation from the collective mind-generated reality is branded aberrant, abnormal, perverted, taboo, and insane, and is treated, corrected, persecuted, and/or punished.

❖

The psychiatric community does not have a definition of insanity, a fact that is quite surprising to a layperson. Sanity and insanity are legal concepts, used to determine whether a person can be held accountable for their actions: sanity means that you know the difference between right and wrong. Mental health professionals just have ever-lengthening lists of neuroses and psychoses codified in their diagnostic manuals; the many ways we can all be crazy.

My dad is a child psychiatrist. I asked him once about the definition of sanity and he laughed heartily. He then described a study done in the 1960s by Roy R. Grinker, Sr., who studied under Sigmund Freud and was emeritus professor of psychiatry at the University of Chicago, University of Illinois, and Northwestern

University. My dad told me, "Grinker looked at a group of college students who had never had any psychiatric issues, who were what any mainstream American would consider completely normal and well-adjusted, yet at the end of the study Grinker threw up his hands and concluded that 'these people were as close as I could come to normality and I still don't know what normal is.'"[14]

"So what's the point of therapy?" I asked.

"To enable a person to be a functioning member of society," my dad replied.

The quintessential mental health professionals—psychiatrists—don't have a concept of sanity. Just functionality. In other words, they're telling us the best we can do is to accept our culture's consensual reality. Our choices are: Accept the reality of our tribe and be considered sane or reject the reality of our tribe and be considered insane.

This is the root of the psychological need to conform, to be a member. Our need to conform is so great that we are willing to accept monstrous beliefs as sane and normal if they are part of our culture's consensual reality.

Sixty years ago, large numbers of German men and women willingly participated in mass murder at the Nazi death camps. Conformity to Nazi social norms allowed them to work hard, raise children, pay taxes, go to church, be a pillar of the community—and be accomplices to the assembly-line slaughter of millions of human beings. They were able to justify their behavior because the Nazi collective mind-generated reality condoned it as both sane and right.

Not long ago, certain Fijian cannibal tribes believed that sexually mutilating their human captives before killing, cooking, and eating them was perfectly normal, sane behavior.

Roman gladiator games two thousand years ago, Salem witchcraft trials four hundred years ago, and Islamic suicide bombers today are all examples of unquestioning conformity to social belief systems that label insane behavior "normal."

As a member of a society we not only agree to believe certain things, we also agree to ignore other things, to deny their existence.

For example, there is evidence that even a limited thermonuclear war could result in the extinction of the human race. Yet the billions of citizens of the nuclear club nations, the United States, Russia,

China, France, England, India, Pakistan, North Korea, and Israel, obviously believe that the preservation of their ideology, political system, and way of life fully justifies risking the total annihilation of the human race.

This truly incredible mind-set, exemplified in the Cold War slogan "Better Dead than Red," has become so much a part of life that most people don't even think about it any longer. The question, "In order to defend your country, are you willing to risk the extermination of the entire human race?" has only one sane answer: "Of course not! If the unthinkable happened *we'd all be dead*, thus without a country and without hope!" The fact that billions of people are willing to live under the threat of self-extinction demonstrates that a chronic state of denial about nuclear weapons and what they represent is commonplace.

Buddhist teacher and psychotherapist Jack Kornfield, in *A Path with Heart*, describes the way our culture agrees to ignore some aspects of life: "To insulate ourselves from the specter of aging and infirmity, we put smiling young people in our advertisements, while we relegate our old people to nursing homes and old-age establishments…We deny death to the extent that even a ninety-six year-old woman, newly admitted to a hospice, complained to the director, 'Why me?' We almost pretend that our dead aren't dead, dressing up corpses in fancy clothes and make-up to attend their own funerals, as if they were going to parties."[15]

❖

If we're born and raised in a lunatic asylum we will adopt the beliefs and mannerisms of the inmates. We can't see the insanity because it's the sea we swim in. There's a cartoon that shows two fish leaping out of the ocean. One is pointing down with a fin and saying to the other, "See? It's called water." All of our reference points for reality are taken from our culture's belief system, so it is almost impossible for us to see that they are not actual reality (whatever that may be), but a mind-generated system of thought *about* actual reality.

Alan Watts, a theologian and scholar of both western and eastern religions, put it this way: "Experiences [of enlightenment or awakening] imply that our normal perception and valuation of the world is a subjective but collective nightmare. They suggest that our ordinary sense of practical reality—of the world as seen on Monday morning—is a construct of socialized conditioning and repression."[16]

Eckhart Tolle uses the word "insane" repeatedly in his best-selling books to describe the human race, both individually and collectively. In *A New Earth* he writes, "One can go so far as to say that on this planet 'normal' equals insane."[17]

To participate in society we must conform; we must assume the collective reality—the madness—of our particular culture. Most of us grow up thinking there is a normal society out there that we can never quite fit into. There is no normal society out there.

3

Delusion and Confusion

We share the beliefs and mind-generated reality of our particular culture, but within that context we create an individual mind-generated reality that delineates a world of our own. We all have our personal delusions.

We've seen how hard it is to see the collective beliefs of our culture. In my experience it's even harder to see our personal beliefs.

Most of us are totally unaware that our perception of reality is a mental construct and extremely limited. Most of us go through life accepting our mind-generated reality as actual reality without any thought of questioning it.

Picture this scenario: Your boss snaps at you. You start imagining that she's angry with you, maybe she's unhappy about that report you turned in last week, the one you knew could have been better, and you work yourself into a state of total panic about losing your job. This is your mind-generated reality.

Then later your boss happens to mention that her in-laws are visiting and driving her completely bonkers. The true cause of her irritability becomes happily evident and your mind-generated reality is revealed to be a fantasy.

Many books, plays, and movies are based on the tensions, conflicts, and farces that arise from people operating out of separate mind-generated realities. In a common story line a character believes that she is in love with someone, but then realizes too late (or just in time) that she actually loves someone else. *Gone with the Wind* is a classic example: through most of the story Scarlett O'Hara's reality is that Ashley Wilkes loves her and she loves him. Only at the very last does she realize the inaccuracy of her mind-generated reality and what clinging to it has cost her.

Our behavior is a direct reflection of our beliefs. One driver will see a snake in the road and take care to avoid hitting it, while another will go out of his way to run over it. To kill or not to kill is completely determined by the belief systems of each driver about the worthiness of snakes. We are and we do what we believe.

Addictions—to alcohol, drugs, eating, sex, shopping, gambling—are enabled by the mind's ability to block out information that does not fit our beliefs. Entire shelves are filled with books documenting the myriad ways people have been "in denial"—that is, deluded—about their addictive behavior. When we are free of the addiction, we look back on that time in our life and ask, "How could I have been so blind?"

How many of us have experienced being delusional in our love life? Usually our friends see our romantic relationships in a much more objective light than we do. A friend may ask, "How can you put up with your girlfriend, she's so boring?" and we'll just shrug it off as if we don't see it—and we don't, in our conscious mind. We block out negative thoughts about our lovers in an attempt to preserve the relationship, so we are oblivious to the problems our friends see. But later, when the relationship is over, we often realize we were aware of the problems all along.

Perhaps the most common delusion of all is the assumption that we know who we are. Ask yourself who you really are. If you are like most people, you will find an abundance of unquestioned beliefs you hold about yourself (I'm pretty, I'm unattractive, I'm smart, I'm stupid, I'm a good person, I'm a bad person, I'm my job, I'm my history, I'm my possessions, I'm my name, etc.), which collectively comprise your identity. All of these beliefs create a mind-generated reality called "this is who I really am." But with sufficient examination you will find that these beliefs in no way reveal the actual reality of your identity. These beliefs are simply what you have been taught and what you have come to believe about yourself.

You might ask: Am I a soul created by God that waited for a particular time and space to be born? If that's true, where was that soul before I was born and where does it go when I die? If there is no God and no soul, am I just an arbitrary combination of genetic material? Is my life just a vehicle for self-replicating DNA to continue a purposeless evolutionary progression? Or, as some physicists suggest, am I just a bunch of subatomic particles randomly banging together, which means my life is an inconsequential blip of consciousness in a completely meaningless universe?

After asking such questions it becomes clear that none of us, ultimately, has any absolute knowledge of *who* we are, *what* we are, *where* we are, *when* we are, *why* we are, *what* we're doing, *where* we came from, or *where* we're going.

These are the kinds of thoughts that keep us up on those dark nights of the soul.

❖

It's not our ignorance of who we are that makes us crazy; it's our delusion that we *do* know who we are that makes us insane.

Every unexamined belief, every unquestioned assumption about reality, is a building block of delusional insanity.

Webster's New Universal, Unabridged Dictionary, a massive compendium of words and definitions, provides only these brief (and circular) phrases to define sanity:

> sane: *free from mental derangement*
> insanity: *a derangement of the mind*
> deranged: *insane*

Here's my definition:

> Insanity: *the confusion of mind-generated reality with actual reality*

Does anyone know what actual reality really is? We perceive all this stuff going on, we have all sorts of names for it and unending beliefs about it, but we have no absolute knowledge of what any of "it" really is. That is to say, no one knows what actual reality is.

There's *one* thing we do know: all of us have the absolute certainty that "something's happening"; experience is occurring.

"Something's happening," whatever that ultimately proves to be, is what I mean by actual reality. Actual reality is what is. Actual reality may currently be a mystery to us but the actuality of the existence of the mystery is not in doubt. If you are reading these words then something's happening: the mystery is absolutely real.

Actual reality is not what we think is, or what we have been taught is, or what we have faith is, or what we hope is, or what we fear is. Actual reality is *what is*. If there are fourteen trillion quintillion universes, and/or if everything is infinite oneness, then that is the actual reality, that is *what is*.

Children's questions have a way of revealing just how little we know about even the simplest facets of reality. Walt Whitman says this beautifully in *Song of Myself*:

> A child said, '*what is the grass?*' fetching it to me with full hands.
> How could I answer the child? I do not know what it is anymore than he.[18]

A sensitive fourteen-year-old girl of my acquaintance was sent to a psychologist because she had continued asking "Why?" long after most children give up on the question (for lack of satisfying answers). She was struggling to find a rock of certainty on which to stand. The help she received? A diagnosis of "existential angst."

In order to get along in this life, most of us act as though we *do* know what's real. This is what makes us insane: we confuse our mental model of reality with reality itself.

We believe our mind-generated reality *is* actual reality.

4

Filters of Reality

Robert M. Pirsig asserted in *Zen and the Art of Motorcycle Maintenance* that "definitions are the foundation of reason."[19]

The purpose of definitions is to bring our individual mind-generated realities about the meaning of a word into closer alignment. Then we have a basis for discussion and analysis. Even if you disagree with a definition of mine it allows you to better understand the point I'm trying to make.

Here are definitions for some important words in this book (note: if a definition in this book isn't attributed to a specific dictionary it's mine):

Ego: *I, me; self-awareness; our personality or self-image.*

Subjective: *our individual point-of-view or perspective; cannot be consistently verified as accurate by an impartial observer.*

Objective: *independent of our individual point-of-view; can be consistently verified as accurate by an impartial observer.*

Our mind-generated reality, our individual conscious awareness, has two components: a *subjective reality* and an *objective reality.*

I'll use the analogy of filters to describe how our mind-generated reality is constructed. The sensory stimulation caused by actual reality (whatever that is) must pass through two filters—a construct filter and an analysis/evaluation filter—before we become consciously aware of it.

The raw incoming data of actual reality first passes through our "portal of awareness." Our sensory apparatus, including our eyes, ears, nose, taste, and touch, delivers a stream of information to our brain. Because of the unique configuration of each person's portal of awareness the content of the information will be different for each of us. For example, you may have better eyesight than I do, and as a consequence will have more visual information delivered to your brain.

Arthur has a much keener sense of smell than I do, and he is always asking me, "what is that smell?" My usual reply is "what smell?" Because there is no olfactory data entering my portal of awareness, this smell doesn't exist for me. That doesn't mean there is no odor: there have been plenty of times when Arthur has found the source of an odor I never smelled.

The data that enters the portal of awareness then passes through the construct program to assemble basic physical reality in our minds: space, time, matter, color, up, down, soft, hard, wet, dry, hot, cold, etc. This processed information forms our mental conception of physical reality. Almost everyone perceives physical reality in basically the same way.

Immanuel Kant, in his 1781 treatise *The Critique of Pure Reason*, addressed the debate about whether reality exists only in our minds (that is, he expanded on Dr. Johnson's kick of the stone). He postulated hard-wired circuits in our brains that create a mental image of physical reality. His "categories of understanding" include quantity, quality, causality, substance, space, and time.[20] They guarantee that we all share a common version of objective, physical reality.

Neuroscientists are now confirming Kant's proposition. David Eagleman writes in his 2011 book *Incognito: The Secret Lives of the Brain*, "Babies, helpless as they are, pop into the world with neural programs specialized for reasoning about objects, physical causality, numbers, the biological world, the beliefs and motivations of other individuals, and social interactions."[21]

Examples of physical reality: rocks are hard unless they're molten; water is wet unless it's frozen or gaseous; and humans have many different skin colors. Imagine a child from an Amazonian jungle tribe brought into a New York apartment. While not having a clue as to the purpose of the computer screen on the table, he would nonetheless respect the physicality of the object: he wouldn't try to put his hand through it.

If you still don't believe in the existence of physical reality, if you think there are only subjective perceptions, if you say "you have your reality and I have mine," I ask: how can you have followed my arguments up to this point? How can we have a conversation about *anything*, unless there is a physical reality that we share, one that forms a foundation of shared concepts? We certainly have our own subjective perception of physical reality, but let's allow that there is a physical reality. Of course we don't know what that physical reality is in the absolute sense, but this is the reality we obviously must accept as we live our lives. Still don't believe? Step in front of the "nonexistent" speeding truck and get back to me on how that worked out.

❖

The mental images of physical reality then pass through the analysis/evaluation filter, which examines and appraises everything based on the criteria of value and meaning: beautiful, ugly, good, bad, useful, worthless, right, wrong, better, worse, important, insignificant, etc. This second filter is what makes us human, and is the source of all creativity and invention, our abstract thoughts, and our reasoning ability.

Animals have a rudimentary version of this analyzing filter, but only a very few are capable of elementary mental abstractions.[22]

The analysis/evaluation filter utilizes concepts, some learned from our culture, some learned from our family, and some created from our own personal experience. The analysis/evaluation filter produces our individual objective and subjective realities.

The analysis part of the filter utilizes objective concepts that allow us to manipulate physical reality: because rocks are hard they make a good building material, the wetness of water can clean the rocks before I use them, and dark skin in humans is an evolutionary response to the greater amount of sunlight in tropical regions. This analysis creates our individual objective reality, which can be consistently verified as true by impartial observers (within limits). Objective reality is composed of *critical judgments* based on utilitarian value, and results in inventions like spears, baskets, alphabets, computers, and space telescopes.

The evaluation part of the filter utilizes personal beliefs and opinions about physical reality: this rock is prettier than the one next to it, that pond-water is disgusting, and people with my skin color are superior. This creates our individual subjective reality, which cannot be consistently verified as true by impartial observers. Subjective reality is comprised of *value judgments* based on our personal perception of meaning and worth. Subjective evaluation determines that some things have more inherent worth or meaning than other things. Subjective reality results in inventions such as art, music, religion, prejudice, and human sacrifice.

The fully processed information, a synthesis of objective reality and subjective reality, is served up to our awareness at any given moment as, simply, "reality." This is what is projected on our screen of awareness. We believe this information to be unfiltered actual reality when in fact it has been heavily processed to form a subjective point-of-view.

For example, imagine a tourist standing at a scenic viewpoint and observing the landscape. His construct filter translates the data of actual reality into: man, standing, looking, viewpoint, cloudy sky, mountain, and river. But then his analysis/evaluation filter applies *value* and *meaning* according to his beliefs: man = me, me = not as good as others who can paint a scene like this; cloudy sky = unattractive because overcast days aren't as pretty as sunny days; mountain = beautiful because mountains are more aesthetically pleasing than flatlands; river = pretty except for that litter on the bank; litter = caused by a lesser-human being who doesn't care about the environment.

This person's mind-generated reality becomes "Beautiful mountain and nice river despoiled by litter flung by an uncaring asshole on a rather unattractive day, with a slightly negative twist because this scene is a reminder of my unhappiness about my non-artistic nature." This is "reality" for our tourist, but it has only a tenuous connection with the objective reality of the scene, and even less of a connection with whatever actual reality might be.

The division between objective and subjective realities is fuzzy, because our subjective beliefs color our perception of everything with judgments of value and meaning. For example, we have a rag rug in our home office. When I look at this rug, I am seeing it through a veil of warm feelings for my great-grandmother who made rugs like this. Our rug is rather plain, but to me it is beautiful because of the memories it evokes. Arthur sees it through another veil: he found it at a used furniture store and is proud of his purchase—it fits this room perfectly. Whenever he looks at the rug, it is more attractive because of this association.

In addition, as we will see, what we think of as objective reality is often revealed to be subjective. However, learning to tease apart the subjective from the objective will help us deal with our insanity.

❖

A belief sounds like a harmless thing. In fact, beliefs completely shape our view of the world and our lives. Actual reality is filtered through our preconceptions before it reaches our conscious awareness. What we call reality is a mental model created by our objective and subjective beliefs. The analysis/evaluation filter is not a passive sifter of information but an active analyzer and arranger of both incoming sensory data and information stored in our memories.

The reason that people perceive reality differently is because every mind interprets reality in a unique way, due to the personalized content of their analysis/evaluation filter, as well as their unique portals of awareness. For instance, imagine two people standing side by side and looking at a particular tree. They may be looking at the same tree, but what they *see* is different.

The first difference in the perception of the tree is caused by the fact that the two people in our example have different portals of awareness; they have different sensory capabilities. One person may see details in the bark that are just a blur to the second; the second may smell the fragrance of the tree while this is completely unknown to the first.

In addition, they cannot share the identical line-of-sight perspective of the tree. Their physical position relative to the tree is necessarily different which means their construct filters perceive the tree differently. These factors usually make a relatively minor difference; most people's construct filters have a lot in common and the end result is a physical reality we all more or less agree to: a tree is almost always a tree.

Our analysis/evaluation filters are far more individualized.

The analysis component involves critical judgment of physical reality. The two observers perceive that this is an oak tree; the leaves are being moved by the wind; this tree is taller than others around it. This forms objective reality; they will probably still be in agreement.

The evaluation of the tree is influenced by everything the two tree-watchers have ever learned, thought, felt, and experienced about the meaning and worth of trees. One may think of "tree" as a miraculous living thing, with individual characteristics and deserving of respect, while the other believes "tree" is uninteresting and valuable only as potential lumber or a source of heat. These are their two subjective realities, and our subjects are much less likely to agree about which of these "realities" is true.

Some examples of objective and subjective realities:

That person is obese: objective reality/verifiable fact. Fat people lack self-control, they're weak and repulsive: subjective reality/unverifiable opinion.

I have a pimple on my face: objective reality/verifiable fact. The pimple makes me unattractive and I have to hide until it's gone: subjective reality/unverifiable opinion.

Some people like to have sex with multiple partners: objective reality/verifiable fact. People who have sex with multiple partners are immoral and evil: subjective reality/unverifiable opinion.

Over the course of human history the analysis/evaluation filter has become clogged with subjective beliefs pretending to be objective facts, mixing constructive analysis like "that river would be easier to cross if we built a bridge," with superstitious beliefs like "sacrificing a virgin will appease the gods and ensure a fruitful harvest." As we've seen, if enough people believe something, it's hard to even recognize it as a belief anymore.

❖

I'd like to spend a little more time looking at the construction of objective reality in our minds because it's tempting to believe that our internal model isn't affected by our beliefs. A tree is a tree, no matter what I believe, right? Our model of objective reality usually matches physical reality enough to allow us to function in the world, but we do not perceive the raw information of physical reality that enters our senses. We perceive only processed information.

We are born with impressive mental processing equipment—our construct filter—but, as we will see, infants must add more. We need to accumulate beliefs in our analysis filter that allow us to correctly interpret sensory stimuli.

Annie Dillard's Pulitzer Prize-winning book *Pilgrim at Tinker Creek* is an extended meditation on what it means to see. After years of walking in the woods and looking closely at tiny creatures, she had never seen a praying mantis egg case. When she learned what to look for she immediately found dozens that she had passed by many times on her daily walks.[23]

Ms. Dillard also describes with wonder the experience of people, blind their entire life, who suddenly gained their vision when cataract surgery was invented in the 1950's. These people didn't immediately see as we do: after the surgery almost everyone experienced great difficulty in perceiving three-dimensions; all they could see when they looked at the world were blobs of colors and varying amounts of luminance.

Those of us endowed with normal vision don't remember learning, while we were infants, that shades of grey define the boundaries of objects. We don't remember learning, through the combined input of seeing with our eyes and feeling with our hands and mouth, what edges and shadows mean.

Ms. Dillard relates how some of the older adults wished they had never had the surgery because, with sight, the world had become too large and confusing. They didn't understand perspective—they couldn't comprehend how things varied in size with distance. One woman would close her eyes whenever she had to negotiate a spatial task such as walking down stairs.

Pawan Sinha, associate professor of brain and cognitive sciences at MIT, is investigating how we learn to see through a humanitarian project called Project Prakash. Blind children in India are given medical treatment to restore their sight. Some of these children are then enrolled in a scientific study to discover how the brain learns to take the raw input of visual information and translate it into a mental image of an object.

Dr. Sinha has found that these children initially perceive images just as those cataract patients did, as regions of different colors and brightness. "The brain has this complex task of putting together, integrating, subsets of these regions into something that's more meaningful, into what we would consider to be objects," Dr. Sinha said in a lecture at a TED conference in November, 2009. "And nobody knows how this integration happens."[24]

Oliver Sacks, professor of neurology and psychiatry at Columbia University and the author of many popular books about the strange workings of the human mind, wrote about learning to see objective reality in *The Mind's Eye*:

> Although seeing objects, defining them visually, seems to be instantaneous and innate, it represents a great perceptual achievement, one that requires a whole hierarchy of functions. We do not see objects as such; we see shapes, surfaces, contours, and boundaries, presenting themselves in different illumination or contexts, changing perspective with their movement or ours. From this complex, shifting visual chaos, we have to extract invariants that allow us to infer or hypothesize objecthood...The world of objects must be learned through experience and activity: looking, touching, handling, correlating the feel of objects with their appearance.[25]

Neuroscientist and artist Beau Lotto gave a TED talk in 2009 entitled "Optical Illusions Show How We See" that illustrates the process Dr. Sacks describes above. One of Mr. Lotto's demonstrations involved a drawing of various geometric shapes. He isolated two sections of the drawing that conveyed exactly the same visual information to the viewer's brain—same shape, size, and color. Then he revealed where these two areas fit into the larger diagram: one was the shaded side of a yellow box while the other was an illuminated side of an orange box. They may have conveyed exactly the same information to my retina, but when I looked at the complete picture I saw different colored boxes, one in shade and the other not. The two surfaces didn't look the same to me, even though I knew they were identical.[26]

Our brains interpret information differently depending upon the context.

Mr. Lotto stressed this as the most important point in his talk:

"The light that falls onto your eye—sensory information—is meaningless, because it could mean literally anything...There's no inherent meaning in information. It's what we do with that information that matters. So how do we see? We see by learning to see."

Clearly, the information about the world that comes in through our eyes does not match the image of the world in our mind. A great deal of mental processing—the analysis of sensory input using beliefs and assumptions—must occur in order for us to decipher visual stimuli into meaningful objects.

Quantum physicist David Deutsch, in his book *The Fabric of Reality*, concludes that our mental processing results in an inaccurate model of reality:

> We realists take the view that reality is out there: objective, physical, and independent of what we believe about it. But we never experience that reality directly...What we experience directly is a virtual-reality rendering, conveniently generated for us by our unconscious minds from sensory data plus complex inborn and acquired theories (that is, programs) about how to interpret them...Since our concepts and theories (whether inborn or learned) are never perfect, all our renderings are indeed inaccurate. That is to say, they give us the experience of an environment that is significantly different from the environment that we are really in. Mirages and other optical illusions are examples of this. Another is that we experience the earth to be at rest beneath our feet, despite its rapid and complex motions in reality.[27]

Some people may still protest that our mental processing allows us to build a model that accurately represents the physical reality right in front of us. This however, is not true. I've already given examples of people not seeing things right in front of their eyes, here's another:

For many years I lived in a small town. A woman who also lived there had beautiful waist-length hair that I (enviously) admired. I was only a casual acquaintance of hers (in a small town you are at least a casual acquaintance of everyone). One day I saw her in a restaurant and her hair was at least a foot shorter; when I exclaimed about her haircut she replied, "Do you know you are the first person to mention it even though I cut my hair a couple of weeks ago? People who work with me every day didn't even notice."

Psychologists Christopher Chabris and Daniel Simons have developed fascinating experiments that demonstrate how easily we can miss aspects of physical reality that are right in front of us. You can experience their most famous experiment yourself: "selective attention test," on YouTube (I won't give any more information because it can only be experienced if you don't know what the experiment is about; I highly recommend you try it, it's an amazing experience).

Chabris and Simons conclude from their experiments that the ability to focus our attention and block out details not relevant to the task at hand is a very important skill that evolution has given to humans. The analysis/evaluation filter looks for patterns and information that will be beneficial to our survival and screens out irrelevant data. This filter, in the researchers' words, is looking at the world with "expectations and goals."

In the book describing the above-mentioned experiments, they write: "Expectations are based on our prior experiences of the world, and perception builds on that experience. Our experience and expectations help us to make sense of what we see, and without them, the visual world would just be an unstructured array of light, a 'blooming, buzzing confusion' in the classic words of William James."[28]

For example, when we are driving, if the red color of the leaves on a tree by the side of the road was as interesting to us as the red brake lights on the car in front of us, we would never make it alive through a day. We have to prioritize and filter.

We do not see actual reality. As these scientists have shown, we don't even see physical reality accurately. Our beliefs, expectations, and inborn and acquired theories filter physical reality to produce an individual mind-generated objective reality.

❖

Because our objective reality is the product of beliefs, it is subject to error and change.

A common example of change in the perception of objective reality is the Copernican revolution. Once upon a time everyone believed that the sun (and everything else up there) revolved around the earth. There was scientific evidence to support this view, in addition to everyday personal observation. Then a Renaissance astronomer named Nicolaus Copernicus presented irrefutable proof that the reverse was true. Suddenly, "reality" changed. Today, we all "know" that the earth revolves around the sun (that is, we take the word of our scientists—personal observation would still convince most of us that the "rising" and "setting" sun revolves around the earth). Reality was not remotely affected by the human race's beliefs about what was going on. Reality was simply what was. The only thing that changed about reality was our beliefs about it.

So-called objective science is affected by the belief-filters of scientists. Alan Lightman describes this effect in *Great Ideas in Physics*: "The exploding star of A.D. 1054, the Crab Nebula, was sighted and documented by the Chinese, but nowhere mentioned in the West, where the Aristotelian notion of the immortality of stars still held sway. We often do not see what we do not expect to see."[29] This is an old example, but science is still being affected by subjective-belief-led fashions in thought.[30]

5

My Story

Another way of looking at the filtration process is to say that we're constantly telling ourselves a story. In the example of the rug in the last chapter, my mind-generated reality of this objective entity involves a story about my great-grandmother. Our tree-viewers told themselves stories about living beings or building materials. We make sense of the world by creating a narrative around everything. I will call this internal storyteller the "subjective mind."

Not only do we build a model of the external world in our minds, we also construct a model of our internal world, which constitutes our self-image. This self-image is the personality, and it can be thought of as the "story of me," or My Story.

Imagine a person named Lee. When Lee enters a room filled with people her mind's objective analysis keeps her from walking into the walls and furniture and confirms the existence of the other people, which allows her to interact with them. However, the way she interacts with those people is completely controlled by her subjective beliefs, which are part of her analysis/evaluation filter.

Psychologists call the effect of beliefs on our perception of reality "cognitive biases." For example: we interpret an event in a way that confirms our preconceptions (confirmation bias) and we reject evidence that contradicts our beliefs (semmelweis reflex).

Let's say that some of the core subjective beliefs Lee formed about herself were these: I'm ugly, I have a good singing voice, I'm a bad dancer, no one could love me, being funny makes me popular. These self-directed value judgments create Lee's self-image. All incoming sensory data and all internal memory data are interpreted in accordance with these beliefs. Lee will be the clown in the room, making the other people laugh, willing to look silly because no one is going to think she's beautiful anyway.

No matter what situation Lee finds herself in, she will interpret it as confirmation that she is ugly, able to sing, graceless, unlovable, and comedic. If Lee is rejected after auditioning for a part in a musical, she will be sure it's because of her looks or her problems with dancing—there's no way it could be due to a lack of singing talent because she's convinced she's a good singer (which might be completely untrue). If a person says to Lee, "I love you," all that she can do is reject the avowal of love because it contradicts one of her core beliefs, "I am unlovable." Lee will think, "He doesn't really love me, he just likes being around me because I make him laugh."

Each of us spends a lifetime starring in the drama called My Story. The plot or theme of My Story is made up of all of the beliefs and value judgments we formed about ourselves at a very early age and continue to act out over our lifetimes.

To illustrate I'll sketch out a few plot lines that have been major defining forces in my life.

My Story includes: I'm smarter than most people, I'm not competitive, I need to please other people in order for them to like me, I'm non-artistic, I like sex too much, and I'm a weak person.

My Story causes me to regularly misunderstand and misinterpret what others say and do because I translate their words and actions into the theme of My Story. I literally do not perceive what they say or do, I only hear and see what fits the plot of My Story. The endless chatter I hear in my head is my mind interpreting everything that happens to me according to the plot line of My Story.

I think I am smarter than most people. I was certainly born with an excellent brain, and was privileged in my upbringing—raised by educated, intelligent, professional parents—and in my education. But I have been arrogant about my smarts: I think I know more than other people about a lot of things, including how to manage their lives. I give advice and then become indignant when the other person doesn't follow it—don't they know how smart I am? I consider myself an intellectual and think this makes me better than most people.

For most of my life I sincerely believed that I was a nice, caring individual who wasn't concerned with winning or being first. Not long ago I had the startling revelation that I am an extremely competitive person. My subjective belief was the opposite of objective reality. I'm actually an aggressive, fierce competitor with one goal in mind: to be number one.

When I was in college I loved to play Othello, a strategy game modeled on the Chinese game of Go. I must have played hundreds of games in those years and I can only remember losing one match. I always ascribed this winning streak to my skill alone (see: "I'm smarter"), but as I think back I can see that I spent enormous energy in the consideration of potential moves that was motivated by a strong competitive nature. Once I went on a first date with a guy who knew of my love for the game. We went to a café with game tables and played Othello. I beat the guy once, then twice, and during the third game considered throwing it to him, but quickly discarded that as contemptible. After my fourth victory we left...and this first date was also the last! The fact that we could play four games in one evening says a lot—there's no way this guy was smart enough for me.

I am very competitive with my husband Arthur. No matter what he does, I have to be able to do it too and do it better than him. Arthur and I quit playing games early in our relationship because he disliked the adversarial feeling that would result. I thought at the time it had nothing to do with me—it was just *his* problem with competition.

At the restaurant where I was manager for a few years I kept the employees in line by example—they were all expected to live up to my model of perfection. No one could do any job better than me.

This fits in with another of my defining beliefs: I have to please others in order for them to like me. I think that only by doing everything perfectly will others find me acceptable.

I also think it's better to do what others want in order for them to like me. One day my college boyfriend said to me, "When I was at a party with my other girlfriend, I could look over at her and know exactly what she was thinking—was she having a good time, did she want to leave, etc. But when I look at you I have no idea what you're thinking." I shrugged it off at the time, but later came to realize that this was because I was hiding my feelings. What I wanted didn't count; it's the other person whose opinion matters.

Again this interlocks with another defining belief: I'm weak; I'm at the mercy of people and events around me. Perhaps this started when I was learning to walk. My brother is eighteen months older than me, and when he saw me standing he loved to push me down. My mother tells me that it got to the point that when I saw him enter the room I would sit down. Some could argue this was proactive, but I have always seen it as the beginning of a passive approach to life. I perceived sitting down as a weakness, as the action of a victim, and that's the way it was written into My Story.

The form my relationships have taken is, "I'm weak and the man is strong"—at least in my mind (which is all the reality I know!). After my three-year college relationship ended, I began a relationship with Arthur, which is now in its fourth decade. Early on, I noticed Arthur did some of the same things I had hated in my college boyfriend. For example, I would be talking to one of them and they would start talking about something completely different. They would act as if they were completely oblivious to the fact that I had been talking.

At first I was outraged when I saw Arthur engaging in these same annoying behaviors, and then I wondered, could this really be a coincidence? Could it possibly be sheer chance that out of the millions of men in this country I had picked two who acted in precisely the same way? Or could it have something to do with me? The latter explanation appeared more likely.

Because I think of myself as weak I unconsciously encourage other people to dominate me. Even when they fail to honor my request, I still misunderstand what they say and do in order to satisfy my need to play weak. For many years of our relationship I felt like a ghost in Arthur's shadow. I blamed Arthur for being the villain. The truth is My Story required a villain. If Arthur weren't here I'd find another man to play villain to my victim. I picked Arthur precisely because he would play this game. I unconsciously stage-manage our relationship to satisfy My Story's plot requirements.

I'm ashamed of being weak because I think it makes me less of a person. I hide it from other people as best I can.

Sex has been a confusing part of my life. I was very shy in high school and had few dates, until one night at a party in my senior year I started making out with a guy who was very popular and had just broken up with his long-time girlfriend. We began dating and our relationship was immediately sexual; our main activity on dates was driving to a remote location and making out. I went directly from not-dating to fellatio. I was very happy...until one night when we were heavily involved in making out and I begged him to fuck me (our sex involved fellatio-to-orgasm for him, but not much to stimulate me). He immediately got up, told me to get dressed, and without another word drove me home. He never spoke to me again. I'm sure part of the reason for his action was his father was a gynecologist. Nonetheless, this was a devastating experience for me. I had discovered that I loved sex, but I added sex to my weakness Story and made sex more about pleasing a man than pleasing myself.

At the same time, I obviously loved sex! In my college years, while my friends quickly settled into monogamous relationships I made it clear to my boyfriend that I wanted an open relationship so I could date—have sex with—other men. And for the next dozen years, including the first decade of my relationship with Arthur, I had some amazing sexual adventures. But I struggled with guilt—a "good girl" shouldn't like sex so much. Sex was a huge source of pleasure, but it also became one of the biggest problems in my relationship with Arthur. He loved my free-spirit attitude toward sex and hated my guilt about it. And of course he had his own issues with sex!

At one point in my life I read a lot of spiritual books, and always I would wait hopefully for some advice on how to see sex from a more enlightened perspective. It always seemed as if the author either ignored sex completely, or did a whitewash of the subject, as if they were as confused as I was.

I have a vivid memory of being a miserable failure in elementary school art class. One day we were told to draw portraits; the teacher let me know (at least that's how I interpreted it) that I had no artistic talent at all. For the rest of my childhood and a good portion of my adult life I operated from the belief that I was not artistic. Ironically, for the last fifteen years I have been making a living through my artistic eye; Arthur and I produce nature videos. One of my favorite hobbies is weaving, and I love creating intricate patterns of color and texture.

As I've grown older I have realized how wrong My Story is: I'm not the smartest person around. I'm not non-competitive. I'm not a weak, cowardly victim. I don't have to please other people in order for them to like me. I'm not a sexual weirdo. I don't lack artistic talent. This is just the Story I told myself. My Story was put together when I was a child to fit into the confusing world I was born into. I thought My Story was the best way for me to play the game of life in order to survive, and I still play variations on this theme every moment of every day.

As I've started to question the beliefs that make up My Story, I've realized how deluded I've been about myself. I was blind to basic aspects of my personality. As long as I was convinced that, for example, my subjective belief "I am not competitive" was an objective fact, I was completely kidding myself. Now that I have exposed this belief as a lie, I may still be competitive but at least I am not so deluded about who I am. (My mother laughed when I told her my big realization about being competitive—apparently the only person surprised by this revelation was me!)

But this illustrates the main point: I have been deluded about reality my entire life. You'd think I would be able to clearly see something as intimate as my own personality, wouldn't you? But I don't. I'm insane: I'm convinced that my mind-generated reality, My Story, is actual reality, when it isn't. I'm out of touch with what is actually true.

❖

Given that everyone is insane, that we all confuse our mind-generated reality with actual reality, it will be useful to distinguish *degrees* of insanity and delusion.

Objective reality may be a mind-generated delusion, but it is based on a critical analysis of physical reality; it is tethered to whatever that "something's happening" turns out to be. Subjective reality is where we can become lost in a world entirely of our own, with no connection to the world outside us.

Our subjective reality is created by the subjective beliefs in our analysis/evaluation filter. These include value judgments like "I'm smarter than you," but they also include value judgments like "subtle browns and reds work well together" that informed Rembrandt's self-portraits.[31]

Subjective value judgments produced the Cambodian killing fields and the Spanish Inquisition; they also bring us art and music.

We make value judgments every moment of every day. When we pick a car out of the thousands available for purchase (when you factor in color and styling options), we base our decision partly on objective critical judgment—price, mileage, carrying needs (do we need 2 seats or 7); but we also base the decision on subjective factors—color, style, sound system, etc. These personal preferences are based on value judgments—I prefer red to green so my cars have mostly been red.

Having value judgments isn't what makes me crazy. What makes me crazy is when I think I am *better* because of my choices; when I think my preferences aren't just personal subjective opinions but are rooted in objective fact. When I think my BMW literally makes me superior to the person who drives a Ford.

The objective/subjective split allows us to differentiate the layers of our insanity. We can then selectively peel these layers like an onion. Subjective reality posing as objective reality is what's making us craziest, what we can peel off first, what I'll call the most extreme expression of our insanity.

Objective reality is our lifeline out of the chaos produced by billions of people babbling their conflicting subjective realities at one another. Objective reality represents something far less distorted—something far more logical and consistent—than subjective reality.

We can restate the definition of insanity using these concepts:

Insanity: *the confusion of subjective reality with objective reality*

Distinguishing between objective and subjective reality is the meaning behind the famous Zen saying, attributed to the Eighth Century Buddhist Ch'ing Yuan [bracketed comments by the author]:

> Before I studied Zen, mountains were mountains and rivers were rivers.
> [My mind-generated reality *is* reality—unquestioned]
> While I studied Zen, mountains were no longer mountains and rivers were no longer rivers.
> [I questioned my assumptions. Everything is mind-generated, both subjective reality and objective reality—therefore nothing is real; all is illusion]

But when I mastered Zen, mountains were again
mountains and rivers were again rivers.
[I now see the difference between objective reality and
subjective reality—and I'm comparatively sane] [32]

I have defined "ego" as the awareness of "I," that is, self-
awareness. Ego is not exclusive to humans. Animals have self-
awareness—they survive by maintaining their self through time. An
ant will move away from a burning match because it is aware that its
body is in danger of being injured by the flame. It is clearly aware of
itself. Even if that awareness is "self = physical body," it is still self-
awareness.

Most humans' current state of self-awareness is self = My Story.

I believe the ego has been unfairly demonized in our culture. It
has been equated with an overly high opinion of one's self,
arrogance, selfishness, self-centeredness, etc.

In many spiritual traditions ego has been seen as the supreme
obstacle to enlightenment, something in need of eradication or
abandonment. The concept of ego-transcendence is held up as an
ideal, but how can I exist without a sense of I? If I have no self-
awareness how can I "be here now" in this dualistic world?

Someone I know once told me about his Samadhi—a peak
spiritual experience of oneness with the All. I was jealous, but I also
noticed that he still had an awareness of self during that experience.
Someone had the experience of the Samadhi (otherwise he couldn't
say "*I* had that experience").

The ego is the point-of-view of consciousness.

Without ego we would not be aware of our existence.

As long as we live in the universe of duality each of us will be a
self; the "I" will exist; we will have an individual point-of-view; we
will have a subjective perception of reality; we will have an ego.

Subjective reality and objective reality are both important (in fact
the division is for convenience; the line between them is fuzzy). I am
not advocating the eradication of subjective reality; the
analysis/evaluation filter has brought us an amazing array of
technological and artistic achievements—from the first stone spears
and bone flutes to the International Space Station and the Museum
of Modern Art. We don't want to throw the baby out with the bath

water.

Our problem isn't that we have a subjective perception of reality. Our problem is that we believe our subjective perception is actual reality.

Sanity, to say the very least, is *not* confusing our subjective reality with actual reality.

If we want to move towards sanity we need to learn how to stop taking our subjective reality for granted and learn how to question the beliefs that create that reality.

The first step towards sanity is to acknowledge our insanity, to admit the simple and obvious fact that we are out of touch with reality. As we'll see, humility is the golden key.

Part Two

We Are All Innocent

6

Why It's So Hard To Change

"Insanity is doing the same thing over and over and expecting different results." This popular quote is often attributed to Albert Einstein.

Why is it so hard to change? Why do I do the same things over and over again, even when I know that doing so hurts me and/or others?

I don't know about you but I hate to admit I'm wrong. The reason I'm so reluctant to admit that I'm wrong is because this requires challenging the foundation of my mind-generated reality: my beliefs.

When we realize a belief is untrue and stop believing in it, we "kill" the belief. Once a belief has been incorporated into our analysis/evaluation (a/e) filter it becomes part of our Story, so when it dies it feels like part of us dies too. To change we have to kill part of us, and that's scary.

A belief becomes part of our a/e filter when we conclude that it is true and beneficial to our survival. Once it's there, it filters reality so we only see what confirms the belief as true. We become predisposed to see only evidence that supports the belief. Even when we see evidence that contradicts the belief, we still have plenty of historical substantiation in our memory banks that it's true, and since we've made it this far, the survival instinct says, "Better stick with what we know."

Even after I had become aware of the existence of the belief, "I'm a weak person," realized it wasn't true, and saw the cost of believing in it, it still took me years to change the way I related to other people.

In order to understand why change is so difficult, we need to first look at the survival instinct.

The logical principles that govern objective reality can be pared down to three essential laws. We'll look at the first two now. Both of these laws are concerned with the survival of form.

1. Exist as form
2. Survive as form

When I use the word "form" I don't mean to imply that I think the physical universe is actually real. I don't know what actual reality is. It may be that the ancient Hindus were right: the universe is *maya* or illusion. What we call physical reality may be a dream, and actual reality may be infinite formlessness. However, as we are obviously stuck in the dream, let's assume that physical reality exists and that we live in a universe filled with an almost endless variety of forms.

The word "form" is a convenient way of talking about what exists in the physical realm. The universe appears to be comprised of separate entities—forms we call galaxies, stars, planets, trees, rats, fleas, and bubonic plague bacteria.

Form doesn't necessarily mean something physical; it means anything that appears to have separate, delineable existence in space/time or thought.

Imagine an apple in a large fruit bowl. A particular apple is a distinct entity, an object that is given its identifiable thus nameable form by virtue of its being delineated by the surrounding "not-*that-apple*"—the air, the adjacent apples, pears, bananas, the fruit bowl, etc. If the bowl contains only seemingly identical, flawless supermarket apples, gleaming with wax and preservatives, the apple on the top is distinguishable from the third apple down on the left by virtue of its position in space and time.

A human being is a form. A slice of apple pie is a form. A crumb of piecrust is a form. An atom is a form.

The two laws are obviously logical and essential: In order to survive you must first exist, and in order to continue to exist you must survive. The driving force of all evolution is survival.

Survival: *the effort of a form to maintain its existent structural integrity.*

In other words, every form or thing in the universe is trying to stay unchanged through time. Logically, the goal of survival can only be immortality. Immortality is the state of eternal changelessness. Every form in the universe is efforting to remain unchanged, exactly as it is right now, forever.

Despite the effort to maintain structural integrity, no physical form in the universe remains unaltered from one instant to the next. If you looked at a diamond through a powerful enough microscope you would see a constant boiling of change at the atomic level. The seemingly durable rock is actually changing across any two consecutive measurable units of time.

A form rightly sees change as the literal death of its present-time manifestation. When a form changes, it ceases to be what it was before the change occurred. The chance of that form ever re-configuring itself exactly as it was before, with every dynamic and/or physical variable precisely the same, is zero. Nevertheless, a surviving form is bound by universal law to resist change as if its very "life" depended on it.

The failure of physical forms to achieve changelessness is sometimes quite subtle and often difficult for us to perceive (particularly for creatures capable of mentally drawing in a friend's moustache on his half-shaved upper lip). Time-lapse photography allows us to see that our seemingly stable world is perpetually changing, and that our ability to perceive this constant change is severely limited.

As much as many of us hate change, we owe a debt of gratitude to the forces of change. A changeless, static universe would be frozen into inactivity and lifelessness. Nothing could happen.

The universe and all it contains is bound to attempt to survive, but it is equally bound to surrender to the inevitability of change. With the seeming exception of *Homo sapiens*, every physical form on this planet gracefully surrenders to change for a very good reason: it has no choice.

One of the things we find so appealing about the wild animal kingdom is the phenomenal degree of acceptance we observe there. A bird clinging to an icy branch during a winter storm doesn't appear to whine or rail against the unfairness of it all. It rides out the storm as best it can; it does all it can to survive. It accepts its existent reality. It is incapable of doing otherwise.

I love to walk on the beach. When I'm at the ocean I spend a lot of time at the high-tide line looking at the interesting remains of creatures deposited there. Over the years I have encountered many dead seabirds in the same posture of complete surrender: lying on their breast, wings extended, their head turned to the side. Once I came across a seagull that must have died just a short time before. I could see the trail the bird left in the sand as it struggled against death, dragging itself up the beach away from the water. Then the trail turned at a 90-degree angle and the bird came to rest in that position of acceptance. The bird looked as if it was in a state of grace; as if it was about to fly off into eternity.

❖

Perhaps the most distinguishing feature of *Homo sapiens* is our ability to whine; to complain; to express non-acceptance with the way things are. Humans don't accept their lot—they do something about it. Prehistoric humans did not accept being barred from the northern latitudes by the cold of winter. They learned to control fire, wear animal skins, and build shelters. We could say that it is dissatisfaction, the absence of acceptance, which is the true Mother of Invention. This lack of acceptance was made possible by the evolution of an entirely new category of surviving form: a "thought-form."

Thought-form: *a mind-generated non-physical entity; concept; belief; abstraction; opinion; judgment.*

A thought-form—a belief—cannot exist in a vacuum. A belief requires a host believer in order to come into existence and survive. Once accepted as true, the belief is "given life" by the believer. The non-physical form now exists and will attempt to survive through time.

The most noteworthy feature of a thought-form is that it has no physical properties and is therefore exempt from those forces of change that constantly alter all physical form. Nevertheless, a thought-form, because it exists, is bound to struggle against any threat to its structural integrity. The only threat to the survival of a thought-form is the conclusive proof of its falsity or limitation. Magellan, the first to circumnavigate the globe, literally killed the thought-form, "the world is flat."

A belief survives as long as the host believer is persuaded that it is absolutely true: that it is not just a belief *about* reality but is, in fact, *reality itself.* The belief says "to believe in me is pro-survival" and "to stop believing in me is death." Interestingly, the belief is telling the truth. To stop believing in it does result in death—the death of the belief.

Every physical form in the universe changes constantly. But a thought-form, unless challenged, can remain unchanged through time. Beliefs can be handed down virtually unaltered from parent to child, through countless generations. A belief can easily outlive a believer.

A thought-form exists as a specific form, which means it must be delineated from every other thought-form. The thought-form "pine trees" and the thought-form "scrambled eggs" must remain separate and distinct lest mental chaos result ("pine eggs" or "scrambled trees"!). However, beliefs interlock to form larger, overarching thought-forms or belief-systems. This adds another dimension to why it's so hard to change.

Let's say a person holds the general belief, "blacks are inferior to whites." This racist concept arose from, and is maintained by, innumerable separate thought-forms (the following are not necessarily true, they are just examples of what might be in a racist's mind): In older movies the bad guy always wore a black hat and the good guy always wore a white hat; black is the color of death; white is the color of purity; black people should be feared because black people commit more crimes than whites; blacks are intellectually inferior to whites; black men have bigger penises than white men.

These individual prejudicial beliefs all work together to support the "truth," thus the survival, of the overarching belief-system.

The influence of our beliefs on our thinking is an unconscious process (the better for the beliefs to survive). We think we see reality clearly and judge circumstances freely, fairly, and objectively because we are completely oblivious to the controlling force of our underlying beliefs. In fact, reality is filtered through the beliefs in our a/e filter before we perceive it, and as a result our vision of reality is skewed to match our beliefs' preconceptions.

Another example: a child starts school and, wanting to be accepted by the Alpha group, adopts the group's belief that the poor children in the class deserve ridicule and contempt. A thought-form, "poor = contemptible," is born. The belief, "poor people are contemptible," will now exercise control over the new believer for the rest of her life, unless it is examined and exposed as the lie that it is.

A thought-form survives by constantly interpreting reality to prove its "truthfulness." Our believer might justify her belief in the contemptibility of poor people by pointing to the high incidence of crime among the poor, while ignoring the obvious ramifications of poverty, the need and desperation that motivate some crimes, and conveniently overlooking white-collar crime—all in order to rationalize the continued survival of her prejudicial beliefs about the poor.

Prejudice takes many forms.

By the time I was in college I had created a hip self-image. I wasn't a conformist square who joined a sorority or participated in other loathsome conventional activities. I was a proud independent and outsider. I was a rebel. In 1979 after my junior year I went on a summer-long trip to the Soviet Union. I traveled with a group of about twenty-five people, most of them my age. One man seemed really conservative and, because I had formed the judgment that square people are uninteresting and not worthy of my time, I never spent any time with him.

Then, the very last day our group was together I happened to be stuck alone with this man at the airport for an hour or so, and I learned that he was a master weaver. Earlier that year I had learned to weave and had fallen in love with the craft. I was sick when confronted with the cost of my prejudice: here was someone with whom, in reality, I shared a very strong interest, someone I could have learned from, and yet I had blown the chance because of my narrow-mindedness. My preconceptions had blocked my ability to see him for who he really was. I believed I knew who he was, and that belief blocked me from learning anything about him.

❖

The relationship of a thought-form to a believer is that of a parasite to a host. The parasite survives via the host's continued belief in it. Obviously, we are the source of our beliefs: we assumed them, we gave them life, and we permit them to survive by continuing to believe in them. While our parasitic beliefs are not literally separate from our host minds, the parasite/host analogy is a convenient way of examining the self-serving nature of thought-form survival, of the deceptive and manipulative nature of surviving beliefs.

Once the host believer has accepted a parasitic thought-form as true, the thought-form exerts control over the host. Rationalization is the way beliefs convince us that they are true and thus beneficial to our survival. Suicide is perhaps the ultimate example of the lengths to which a belief will go in order to survive. A suicidal belief, "Death is preferable to life," will, in order to survive, literally encourage its host to self-annihilate before allowing itself to change/perish.

For a parasite, the optimum state of survival is one in which its host is completely unaware of its existence. The rats in the attic survive much better by gnawing the house down quietly. Once their presence is discovered, the owner will likely call in an exterminator. In human beings, our parasitic beliefs are invisible because they have convinced us that *they are us*.

Once a thought-form is accepted as true it becomes part of our analysis/evaluation filter: we see a reality distorted by the "corrective lens" of the belief.

There are two types of surviving thought-forms: objective facts and subjective beliefs. An objective fact can be consistently verified as true or factual by an impartial observer. A subjective belief is a personal opinion that cannot be consistently verified as true by an impartial observer.

Imagine this objective fact: a painting of Elvis Presley on black velvet is hanging on the wall in front of me in the lobby of a Las Vegas hotel. This fact is readily verifiable by anyone. Maybe that child from the Amazon wouldn't know who Elvis was, or know the name for the material, or know what a painting was, but he would verify the objective fact of an object hanging on the wall which contains a representation of a man.

Subjective beliefs about the Elvis painting, on the other hand, would vary enormously, from the art connoisseur actually gagging with revulsion, to the irreverent soul with a taste for unintentional satire beaming with devilish delight and demanding the purchase price (with dreams of hanging it in his gallery of bad taste), to those who stand in muted reverence (as others would on beholding a Rembrandt), dreaming of it adorning the wall of their living room.

As we have seen, objective facts can be revealed to be erroneous subjective beliefs—for over a thousand years before Copernicus a widely-accepted scientific theory described how the sun, stars, and planets revolved around the Earth. This theory could predict observed planetary movements very precisely. "The earth is the center of the universe" was a firmly established fact until the day it was proven to be a deeply flawed belief.[33] The line between objective and subjective can be hard to draw. Nevertheless, the distinction is useful if we want to do something about our insanity. Remember our basic distinction: objective facts can be consistently verified by an impartial observer while subjective beliefs cannot.

Our minds are programmed from birth with both objective facts and subjective beliefs. These thought-forms configure our mind-generated reality. Most importantly, *our minds store both categories of thought-forms as if they were equally true.* Valuable survival-enhancing objective fact data and long-standing cultural superstitions and prejudices (subjective beliefs) are given equal credibility, each demanding our unquestioned obedience. How to walk, tie our shoes and wipe our nose is psychologically imprinted with the same legitimacy as Santa Claus is real, when we touch ourselves down there the saints cry, boys don't play with dolls, and failure to believe in God will send us to hell forever.

"Walking under a ladder brings bad luck" and "two plus two equals four" are both thought-forms. The difference between these thought-forms is that, under objective examination, one will perish and one will survive. Objective analysis will never substantiate the validity of the belief "walking under a ladder brings bad luck" (other than understanding the likely source of the superstition: it's dangerous to walk under a ladder that might fall, the person on the ladder might drop something, etc.). Conversely, "two plus two equals four" can be readily and consistently verified by anyone at any time at any place.

Most people agree that objective judgment is more credible than subjective opinion. "Objectivity" means careful and unbiased analysis of the facts. A subjective belief survives, therefore, by *pretending* to be objective when it is anything but. Every subjective belief is prejudiced and biased, but presents itself as completely objective in order to be accepted and to survive unchanged.

If we can begin to entertain the idea that a surviving thought-form, even though it has no physical properties, nonetheless attempts to survive with all the tenacity of a cornered rat, that it is a parasite which controls us by becoming a distorting filter of our reality, then we can begin to see which category of thought-form most contributes to our delusional insanity and most fears critical examination. Which of these surviving thought-forms would be most willing to hop up on the examination table under those very illuminating lights of objective inquiry: "Whites are inferior to blacks" or "e=mc²"?

❖

In order to exist and survive, every form has a "primary survival identity," no matter how rudimentary. The ant we threatened with a match earlier had a sense of self to protect. Of course it seems ludicrous to assign the pronoun "I" to an ant, but where else can the survival motivation come from, other than a sense of self? Otherwise, why act to perpetuate existence? The effort to survive as form presupposes a sense of "I am." As evolution proceeds, this sense of self becomes more complex and more conscious.

Many animals have a fairly sophisticated sense of self. Our dogs know when we are mad at them. Our cats can manipulate us into doing what they want. Chimpanzees get angry at visitors observing them in the zoo. This explains why the introduction into the wilds of animals raised in captivity is so difficult: their primary survival identity is no longer that of an undomesticated animal. They literally do not know how to behave in the wilds. A parrot that had spent its life in a cage in someone's living room, and thereby lost its primary survival identity as "wild parrot," probably wouldn't survive long outside the cage.

The primary survival identity of human beings is My Story, our personal amalgam of objective and subjective beliefs; what I've called the subjective mind. In the following chapters I will say things like "the subjective mind is trying to survive," or "the subjective mind hates this." This is just a shorthand way of speaking; I could say something like "the subjective beliefs that are part of my a/e filter make that person seem repulsive to me"....but that would get a bit cumbersome.

As long as we identify with the subjective mind it is our primary survival identity, and as a consequence subjective mind's survival is equated with our survival.

7

The Mask of Assumptions

Every thought-form that comprises my subjective mind is there because it has convinced me that it is true and that believing in it will help me to survive. Thus, "My eyes are blue" (an objective fact) and "I'm weak" (a subjective belief) present themselves as equally true and equally survival-enhancing. The only difference is that one thought-form is based on objective verifiable fact while the other thought-form is based on subjective, biased opinion.

How is the subjective mind formed?

The main task of a newborn is to mentally arrange the world into an orderly, predictable environment in which to survive and participate. Infants must learn to see reality in a way that aligns with the family and cultural environment in which they find themselves.

An infant must first build an objective model of external reality in his or her mind. This model must conform to the mental constructs of those around us. We all need to learn how doors and stairs and toilets look and work. Failure to learn and conform to the rules of objective reality results in the inability to participate fully in life.

Objective reality needs to be built before subjective reality can begin to operate. The subjective realm value-judges the objective realm, so the objective realm must exist in order to be evaluated. The baby must first recognize the distinct and separate entity called "cat" before the post-scratch value judgment "cats are bad" can be formed.

Along with the increasing awareness of being a separate entity, being a boy or girl, and having blue or brown or green eyes, babies begin to assimilate the subjective value judgments of the people in their environment: eating my strained carrots means I'm good, smearing my poo-poo on the bathroom wall means I'm bad, playing cute for my parents' friends means I'm a little angel, and hitting my baby sister means I'm naughty and may not get a visit from Santa Claus.

Survival demands that infants be indoctrinated into their culture's model of reality. A baby's senses soak up its environment like a sponge, taking in subjective belief data right along with objective fact data. Because all of the adults around a child are insane—they all confuse subjective beliefs with objective facts—they express their subjective opinions to the infant as though they were objective facts.

Consequently, the infant mind stores objective fact data and subjective belief data as though they are equally valid, equally objective, and equally pro-survival. The analysis that builds objective reality is clearly pro-survival: we learn to walk, talk, and use the toilet. We learn the ways of the physical world and how to operate within it.

The world of subjective beliefs is another realm entirely. The subjective mind constantly strives to assess self-worth on an ever-teetering seesaw of insecurity, which rocks back and forth between pride and shame.

In order to define "me" as a person who is separate and distinct from everyone else, I incorporated the subjective value judgments of my family and culture. My objective reality says, "I have brown hair." This, however, is not enough to define *me*—lots of people have brown hair. My subjective reality says, "My hair is a dull shade of brown, not as lustrous as other's, but my hair is curly and curly hair is prettier than straight hair." By making subjective value judgments about every conceivable aspect of myself, I define—thus create—my unique identity. Every value judgment I assume about myself becomes a surviving belief, a self-estimation of my worth. Even the color of my hair is a statement of my worth—if I am insecure enough about it, I will dye it to make me "better."

The subjective mind is a life-long critic, an inner voice that's constantly evaluating and judging every moment of our existence.

The subjective mind is what separates us from the wild animal kingdom. We share with wild animals the realm of objective facts produced by analysis of physical reality: a sense of self, a sense of flight and fight, a sense of hungry and full, and a sense of sexual arousal, etc.

The fact that wild animals do not worry about the next day, or wonder whether or not their lives are fulfilling, or obsess about whether their coats are lustrous enough, or feel bored, or seek immortality by mighty deeds or accumulated possessions, or wallow in guilt and regret, or feel embarrassed or insecure, indicates the absence of a subjective "value-meter."

There were five children in my family and as is usual in large families we all had our roles. I was the "'intellectual" and my younger sister the "animal lover." But I interpreted this to mean that I wasn't an animal lover, therefore I (the competitor) felt inferior to my sister. I wanted to excel in everything! As a consequence, I felt I needed to prove my worth in the animal-lover category; I needed to show that I loved animals just as much as my sister. Since we already had a dog and two cats, something smaller was required and a gerbil was the pet I was allowed to have.

The only problem was that I hated gerbils. But since I had to prove myself, I convinced my mother to buy me one of the nasty little rodents. A couple of days later, I let Herman (named after the British band Herman and the Hermits) out of his cage so he could run around my room. He immediately ran down a hole in the closet floor, never to be seen again. My private fear was that Herman was aware of my dislike and got away from me, the animal-hater, as quickly as possible. Of course I didn't breathe a word of this fear to my mother, who was willing to buy me a replacement. This one I didn't let out of its cage (and I can't even remember naming it).

One day my mother called me aside when I got home from school. Sternly leading me up to my room, she wordlessly pointed to the gerbil cage. There lay the gerbil—dead—killed by my neglect. The water and feed tubes were completely empty. The proof of my hatred for animals was fully confirmed. What horror! I had set out to prove my worth and ended up proving my lack of it! Not only was I *not* an animal-lover, I was an animal *killer*.

❖

The human ego is a Frankenstein personality created by our attempts to distinguish our self from every other self. It's a hodgepodge of inherited, borrowed, and invented bits and pieces.

And we *must* build this creature, this separate sense of self, in order to survive. This process of identity building is perhaps the chief source of childhood fears. In fact, this may well be what the "bogeyman" is.

Bogeyman [*Webster's*]: *an imaginary evil character of supernatural powers, especially a mythical hobgoblin supposed to carry off naughty children.*

The bogeyman may be the subjective mind reaching the stage where it's powerful enough to make its presence known to (and ultimately take control of) our awareness. As babies we operate almost exclusively from objective reality. The subjective mind develops quickly, however, and as toddlers we begin to become aware of its presence. We perceive it as an intruder. The awareness of this intruder often comes at night, in the dark, in nightmares, when the distractions of the day are absent. The feeling is that something or someone is *coming to get us.*

Imagine the bogeyman as the subjective mind coming to take us away from our newly created sense of objective self and objective world—both largely uncolored by subjective value judgments. A baby has no sense of good and bad, everything just *is.* Everything is inherently interesting. A child naturally fears the confusion inherent in the new subjective realm.

As toddlers we feel the clean, rational, and predictable world of objectivity slipping away from us. The bogeyman of subjective mind takes us into a new world that is all about pretense and pride, shame and blame, compromise and conformity, prejudice and bias, a world freighted with local morals and half-baked superstitions that we must accept without question or objective proof. This is a world of uncertainty and forced blind acceptance of contemporary dogma.

It is terrifying, because, as we enter the subjective mind's world, we sense that we will never again enjoy the comfort of comparative certainty that the objective realm provided us.

The bogeyman is known throughout the world as a monster that disposes of naughty children. While it's tempting to think of this only as a parental control tactic, I think that's missing the significance of what's happening in the child's mind.

The bogeyman was not created by adults; it is very real to a child; the parents just exploit this fear to manipulate the child to do what they (the parents) want.

No longer is life a simple matter of "I am." Now it is a question of I am good, I am bad, I am right, I am wrong, I am inferior, I am superior, I am pretty, I am ugly, I am smart, I am stupid, I am an animal lover, I am an animal hater, I am naughty, I am nice. This is all subjective mind talk: a persistent evaluator of our worth and a persistent distorter of "I am" (and of all objective reality).

Objective reality rests on a foundation of comparative certainty: "I am" is, observably, a consistently verifiable reality. The value judgments of the subjective mind, on the other hand, are like shifting sand. "I am good" or "I am bad" are in a perpetual state of flux, changing from moment to moment depending upon endless variables. There is no certainty and there is no consistency. Sometimes our parents said "What a good girl!" and other times "No, bad girl." You can be sure we were often confused about what we had done that was bad or good, particularly when we were very young.

The culture from which we draw the values that make up our subjective mind regularly changes its standards of good and bad and right and wrong. There is no objective standard for beautiful or ugly. In the nineteen-fifties women with heavy, voluptuous bodies were considered beautiful, but a scant ten years later in the "Twiggy" era Marilyn Monroe would have been considered too fat to be successful as a model.

John Merrick, the Elephant Man, is thought by many to be the "ugliest" man to have ever lived. In David Lynch's masterful film treatment of Mr. Merrick's life, we are at first terrified at the freak we are about to confront, then we are repulsed by what we see, and finally we begin to experience what underlies this terrible disfigurement: a helpless victim and a kind, gentle, and beautiful human being. The deformity becomes less important than the inner quality of the man. Although initially revolted by his frightening appearance, we begin to see his humanity and to understand the horrors he has suffered. Through compassion we accept his disease and are able to see the man and not his superficial appearance.

By the end of the film we have come to see Mr. Merrick as a beautiful person, while those physically normal people who have exploited him and treated him cruelly have been rendered ugly (and, though the filmmaker does not ask it of us, with compassion even their "ugliness," born of ignorance and insanity, would disappear).[34]

Beauty, as well as ugliness, is truly in the eyes—that is, the subjective mind—of the beholder.

We all confuse our subjective opinions with objective fact. We are all rendered insane in the process.

❖

As we mature our subjective beliefs harden in place, becoming rigid assumptions about reality. "Assumption" means something taken for granted. We're so sure our beliefs about reality are true we don't question them. We take it for granted that we are ugly, or an animal-hater, or naughty, and live our lives as if these assumptions are the truth of the universe.

Our analysis/evaluation filter is made up of assumptions about reality. By the time we reach adulthood we are walking assumptions and by the time old age hits those assumptions have long been encased in concrete.

Subjective mind accepts change only when it is confronted with irrefutable proof that one or more of its beliefs are not true. For instance, when we are young and out on our own for the first time, many of us don't believe that the electric company would be uncaring enough to turn off our lights just because we don't pay our bill. These are *our* lights, and we're special—Mom always told us so! With experience, as most of us become reconciled to the painful reality that the power company *will* turn off our lights, we change our assumption from "I can ignore paying the light bill because I'm special" to "I have to pay the light bill on time."

This type of assumption is the exception. Most of our assumptions are never called into question because they remain purposefully hidden from our own objective observation. These assumptions influence our mental processing without our being aware of their existence (a parasite's delight).

One of the cognitive biases mentioned earlier was "confirmation bias." This well-documented thinking error means we seek out evidence to support our beliefs, while dismissing and distorting any evidence that challenges our beliefs.

I've stayed away from politics in this book as it is a subjective-belief minefield. But it provides a great example of confirmation bias; you could easily argue that this bias is what is undermining our contemporary political discourse. The Internet has made it easy for people to get all their information from one point-of-view. If you're a conservative, you can get all your information from FOX News and the Drudge report. You will feel completely justified in thinking that liberals want to bring about a socialist nightmare. Conversely, if you're a liberal you can get all your information from MSNBC and the Huffington Post and be bewildered why the conservatives want to destroy America.

I like political cartoons, and look at a variety of them everyday. I'm a liberal and the conservative cartoons are like a window into another world; it often takes me some time to comprehend what the cartoonist is even talking about (sometimes I never figure it out). The cartoonist's conservative political assumptions are unknown to me.

Hypnosis is a splendid example of how underlying assumptions work. The hypnotist provides a temporary assumption—the posthypnotic suggestion—that proceeds to exert control over the subject's behavior. Under the spell of hypnotic suggestion, people can be led to do the most surprising things.

The hypnotist might give a subject this instruction: "You will experience that I have halitosis." When the hypnotist approaches him and begins to speak, the subject jerks his face away to avoid the "bad breath." The subject subjectively experiences that the hypnotist has bad breath when that experience has no basis in objective reality. The assumption, the hypnotic suggestion, is controlling the subject's behavior but is entirely unknown to his conscious awareness. If asked why he turned his head, the subject might reply something like, "I thought I heard a noise over there."

A fascinating set of experiments called "split-brain research" showed that our conscious mind weaves a story to rationally explain our behavior to ourselves, and that this story often has no connection to the actual motivation behind a behavior. In the 1960's some people with severe epilepsy underwent a radical surgery; the connection between the two brain hemispheres was severed. When the connection is cut there is a split in conscious awareness: the scientists could show an image to one side of the brain and the subject would not be consciously aware of seeing that image, but the image would still affect the subject's subsequent behavior.

For example, the researchers would show the word "walk" to the non-conscious side of a subject's brain. The subject would then get up and walk, and when asked why, would give a rational explanation: "I wanted to get a drink," or "I needed to stretch my legs." They never said, "I don't know," which was the truth.[35][36]

In the same way, the underlying assumptions that determine our everyday behavior are unknown to us.

The explanations we give to ourselves for our assumption-dictated behavior are often not the truth, because we are unaware of the workings of our subjective minds. We weave a story, My Story, to try and make sense of the often-inexplicable behavior of ourselves and other people.

In the past I often lied to Arthur. I would hide things from him, like a bounced check, because I knew he would get angry. I didn't want anything to interfere with my "Ms. Perfect" image. But the story I would tell myself about why I lied didn't have anything to do with me; it was all about Arthur and his temper.

Once I got a job at a restaurant in a resort town. At the end of the first season, I said to the owner, "Things would go a lot smoother if you had someone in charge of the dining room." She replied, "I have been thinking the same thing, and the job is yours." The next spring when we were getting ready to open for the season, the owner and I got together to discuss salary. Since this was a newly created job, there was no precedent for salary and only an estimate of what kind of time would be involved. Arthur and I had discussed the issue beforehand, and he thought $75 a week was what I should get. But in the meeting I was incapable of asserting my value, which could be seen as patently insane since my capabilities had brought this job into existence! (Did I mention I'm weak?) The owner suggested $50 a week and I took it without even suggesting anything higher.

I told myself that there were a lot of uncertainties, that maybe the job wouldn't require much extra work (I'd be waiting tables also), that this was probably a fair price.

But when I got home I told Arthur I was going to be paid $75. I knew—that is, my mind-generated reality said—that if I told him the truth he'd get mad at me for being such a weakling and we'd have a fight. I also knew that since I did all the finances he'd never find out, so it was a lie I could get away with.

The story I told myself said, "I lied to Arthur because he couldn't handle the truth." The real reason I lied was because I was ashamed of my weakness. I was embarrassed about my inability to negotiate with my employer. The explanation I gave myself for my action was a distorted version of reality. And notice that the story I spun protected myself from harsh assessment while making Arthur the villain.

❖

The word "personality" is derived from the Greek word *persona*: literally, *an actor's facemask*. Visualize creating a papier-mâché mask of your face. To make such a mask, strips of paper dipped in paste are layered one on top of another, using your face as a mold. Imagine that each strip is a single belief about reality created in the mind-programming process of infancy. Each strip is an individual assumption about reality. Each strip is either a subjective belief or an objective fact.

As the strips crisscross they create an overlay: a self-image distinct from our original awareness, both concealing it and distorting its ability to see clearly. The underlying, original identity is buried alive. We begin to identify with the mask. We come to believe that who we are *is* the mask: a mass of dried, hardened assumptions about reality.

Our ego-mask is like a suit of armor that we wear all the time. Even when we're with our friends we keep this suit on; with our lovers we may take off some of the armor but we retain a thinner layer of chain mail underneath.

The ego-mask is comprised of "strips" of objective facts and subjective beliefs. As I've said, this book is not concerned with questioning objective physical reality. Instead we want to expose the beliefs that comprise the subjective mind and its value judgments. These strips produce the craziness that is the source of most of our problems.

In Stanley Kubrick's film "2001: A Space Odyssey," the HAL 9000 computer attempted to take control of the mission by murdering the crew. Dave, the lone survivor, deactivated select components of the HAL 9000 to prevent further mayhem. He carefully unplugged only the section of the computer that was capable of causing more trouble, while leaving the basic regulatory circuits untouched.

In the same manner, we want to identify and unplug only that part of our mind's filtration system that is the immediate source of our insanity: subjective beliefs.

8

Subjective Mind's Greatest Invention

Everyone has innumerable subjective beliefs, many of them highly individual. However, there are a couple of subjective beliefs that are both widely shared and the source of enormous problems.

The first one I'll address is the belief in free will. Free will means the ability to freely choose our thoughts and deeds, without external coercion of any kind.

Free will is a foundational pillar of our culture's collective reality. For many people it is self-evident that free will exists: they experience themselves as self-determined creatures and not pre-programmed robots. Many believe that it is free will alone that separates human beings from the wild animal kingdom. The foundation of Judeo-Christian theology is the belief in free will, beginning with the fable of Adam and Eve. Many philosophers, otherwise meticulous in their thinking, will dismiss convincing evidence that free will does not exist by making totally illogical pronouncements such as, "Free will must be true because life without free will would not be worth living."

I've heard people say, "I feel like I have free will so it must be true." I feel that the sun rises every day, but does that mean the sun revolves around the earth? No.

As we've seen, beliefs that form part of a collective reality can be very difficult to delineate, because there is so much agreement that they are true. You may feel some resistance due to this strong cultural programming, but let's question the belief in free will.

In a court of law the question of free will rests on whether the person on trial is sane. If we are all insane, could free will exist? How can someone who is deluded about reality, who is not perceiving reality accurately, be capable of free choice?

If my subjective beliefs distort my perception of reality to match My Story, how can it be accurate to say I'm acting with free will? The truth is I'm acting according to the programming of my a/e filter. When I asked my mother for a gerbil, was I acting from free will? Did I really want a gerbil? No, I was trying to disprove a belief that existed only in my mind ("my sister loves animals more than me"), but at the time I was completely unaware of my motivations. If I don't know the source of my motivations, how can I be in control?

Is free will another one of our delusions?

What is freedom? If you look the word up in a dictionary you will find many variations on the theme of "absence of constraint." I've condensed these meanings into the following definition:

Free: *unrestrained by limitation.*

This definition of "free" expresses the meaning that most of us associate with freedom. We say things like, "you're free to do as you wish." That means, "you're unrestrained, you can choose anything." But is this possible? Is there any time when there are no constraints on our thoughts and behavior? Is there anyone who is truly free to do as they wish?

Webster's defines "free will" as: *the freedom of decision or of choice between alternatives; the freedom of the will to choose a course of action without external coercion, but in accordance with the ideals or moral outlook of the individual.*

What this definition makes clear is that the meaning of "free will" is based on a relative sense of the word "free." As long as there isn't someone standing over us with a gun forcing us to do something, we're free, even though our choices are still limited by the contents of our minds. Proponents of free will claim we are completely free to choose within a range of alternatives created by our ideals and moral outlook.

By the very definition "free will" isn't really free; our choices are constrained by limitations. What types of limitations constrain our freedom?

Free will means that a person has the ability to choose between realistically possible alternatives; to say I have the free will to fly to Alpha Centauri is absurd. I'm limited in this example by the limits of human technological development. If we bring the example down to earth, what are more ordinary limitations on my choices?

I can't have the free will choice to be an Olympic-class sprinter. I'm limited by my physicality.

I can't have the free will choice to be a famous painter. I'm limited by my artistic ability.

I can't have the free will choice to start a job as a biochemistry professor. I'm limited by the decisions I made in my past.

When we start looking at the question of free will, it becomes obvious that the limitations imposed by my physicality and my mental programming exert enormous constraints on me. Maybe there isn't someone standing over me with a gun, but with all these constraints how can it be in any way meaningful to say I'm free?

In addition, the dictionary definition seems to say that free will depends on the existence of conscious choice. To be able to freely choose between alternatives would require that I be consciously aware of all the alternatives available to me. Free will requires that my actions be the direct result of my conscious choices.

Recent discoveries in neuroscience show that the belief that we have conscious control of our actions is largely an illusion. In reality we are constantly constrained by subconscious forces along with the pressures of our environment.

For example, a study of judges in Israel who spent all day reviewing requests for parole revealed that sixty-five percent of requests were granted right after the judges had eaten, dropping steadily to zero just before the judges' next meal. Given these statistics, does it make sense to say that these judges exercise free will in their estimation of the inmates' qualifications? Or is it more likely that they are limited by their animal nature, getting more critical the hungrier they got? If you asked the judges about their decisions, do you think they would be aware of this tendency to get grumpier as they got hungry, or do you think they would believe they were being equally neutral and fair throughout the day? I suspect the latter would be the case: the story they would tell about their job would be that they approached every case with an equal impartiality.

This study was cited in Daniel Kahneman's bestselling book about the latest research into the workings of the human mind, *Thinking Fast and Slow*. Dr. Kahneman discusses many studies involving "associative thinking" (for example: think of banana and vomit, now try to think of a banana without feeling slightly sick) and "priming" (think of yellow, now think of a fruit—you probably thought of a banana because you were primed with the idea of yellow). Dr. Kahneman concludes, "Studies of priming have yielded discoveries that threaten our self-image as conscious and autonomous authors of our judgments and our choices...The main moral of prime research is that our thoughts and our behaviors are influenced, much more than we know or want, by the environment of the moment." This research is profoundly upsetting to many people, Kahneman says, because it threatens their "subjective sense of agency and autonomy."[37]

In *Incognito: The Secret Lives of the Brain*, David Eagleman, a neuroscientist at the Baylor College of Medicine, argues that free will cannot exist. After establishing that most of the brain's processes operate at a subconscious level, and that our actions, emotions, and perceptions are determined by our genetics, social conditioning, and experience, Mr. Eagleman concludes that "we are driven to be who we are by vast and complex biological networks. We do not come to the table as blank slates, free to take in the world and come to open-ended decisions. In fact, it is not clear how much the conscious *you*— as opposed to the genetic and neural you—gets to do any deciding at all."[38]

Eckhart Tolle argues that free will is an illusion in *The Power of Now*: "Nobody *chooses* dysfunction, conflict, pain. Nobody *chooses* insanity ...It always *looks* as if people had a choice, but that is an illusion. As long as your mind with its conditioned patterns runs your life, as long as you *are* your mind, what choice do you have? None. You are not even there."[39]

If the motivation for an action comes from a subconscious stimulus of which I am completely unaware, how can I say I acted with free will?

I don't have the free will choice to be happy. I'm limited by subconscious beliefs that I'm not aware of that control my reaction to events. I never choose to be happy. I don't wake up in the morning and decide, "today I'll be happy all day long." I just sometimes realize, "I'm happy." And often I have absolutely no idea why.

I don't have the free will choice to fall in love. I'm limited by subconscious forces that attract me to certain people that are beyond my ability to fully understand. I don't choose to be in love, or to fall out of love. What does happen: at certain moments I realize I am in love with someone, or that I'm no longer in love.

I don't have the free will choice to get angry. I'm limited by subconscious forces that operate faster than my conscious mind. I don't choose to get angry; in fact usually I'm not aware of the process of getting angry; all of a sudden I just *am* angry.

One day I was thinking about some of the murderous battles that took place during the Civil War, and wondering what could possibly motivate soldiers to charge up a hillside knowing that the chance of being shot was almost one hundred percent. It occurred to me that maybe we aren't as conscious as we like to think we are. This phrase came to me:

> We consistently *overestimate* our level of consciousness.
> We consistently *underestimate* our level of unconsciousness.

The dictionary definition of "free will" ends with: "The freedom of the will to choose a course of action...in accordance with the ideals or moral outlook of the individual." But as we've seen, the greatest burden of limitation always comes from *within* our own minds! It is literally our own rigid and unbending subjective beliefs that consistently dictate our course of action at any given moment. If I believe I'm ugly, I will *act* and *be* ugly. As long as this belief remains unexamined, I will never be free from my "ugliness" and I will go through life as an ugly person. I will dress and behave exactly in accordance with my ugly-self-estimation. "I'm ugly," a subjective belief, will have every bit as much validity in my mind-generated reality as the objective fact that "birds have feathers." "I'm ugly" will be part of my a/e filtration system and I will never be able to experience life without it (even if I struggle for a lifetime trying to convince myself and others that I'm *not* ugly). I will never be free to have the choice to be a model or enter a beauty contest.

By "acting in accordance with our ideals or moral outlook," that is, in accordance with our subjective beliefs, we are completely constrained and controlled by them.

So far I've talked about internal factors that constrain our freedom. But who would claim to be unconstrained by external forces?

Our job, our school, our police, our peers, our teachers, our taxes, our customs, our weather, our gravity, our family, our neighbors, our wars, our illnesses, our God, our time, our parents, our past, our income, our education, our country, our tribe, our social status, our children, our universe, our ignorance of it, and our approaching death, combined with factors like our intelligence, our psychology, our weight, our appearance, our complexion, our genes, our health, our age, our sex drive, our philosophy, our gender, constitute the steel bars which define our cage of limitation. Every category of belief, relationship, psychology, and physicality exerts a steady and relentless control over us, and therefore a constant constraint.

❖

There's a famous Jesuit saying, "Give me the child for seven years, and I will give you the man." In other words, a person is shaped for life by the time they are seven years old. If you doubt this claim, watch the amazing "Up Series" by documentary filmmaker Michael Apted. In the early 1960's a British television production company gathered twenty seven-year-old British schoolchildren from different socio-economic classes and interviewed them about their lives for a BBC show called "7-Up." Mr. Apted chose fourteen of the original subjects and returned to interview them every seven years. Each film (the latest is "56-Up") contains clips from the earlier films so you can see each person as they mature. It is startling to see how fully the seven-year-old foretells the middle-aged personality.[40]

There are many different theories of childhood development, but most agree that the personality is dependent on a person's progression through stages of psychological development.

One well-accepted theory of personality was developed by Erik Erikson.[41] In his view, the first stage of development involves the child learning trust. Say a baby is born into a family where the parents are both alcoholics who neglect their child and slap her when she cries. This baby learns that she can't trust anyone. This will be a foundational component of her personality, and will affect her ability to form relationships for the rest of her life.

When this person is an adult who cannot maintain a long-term relationship, isn't it preposterous to believe it is her free will choice to be single? Or to believe that the baby made a free will choice to decide that she shouldn't trust others?

When we think about it, could any of us imagine that an infant or toddler is consciously aware enough to make life-defining decisions in a free, rational, carefully considered manner? Instead of imagining a baby lying in her crib making free will decisions about the way she's going to play the game of life, isn't it much more sensible to see an organism whose self-defining decisions are the product of a mechanistic stimulus-response interaction between her psychological/physiological configuration and her environment?

This organism is bound to select what it deems to be the most survival-enhancing option. No matter what a person does later in life, the beliefs that form the foundation of a personality were adopted because they seemed to the child to be pro-survival. No baby ever consciously decided in the crib to grow up and rape children or rob banks, or gossip, or cheat on their wife, or betray a friend, or hate themselves.

❖

Many people, even those sympathetic to the idea that free will is a myth, have trouble understanding why I think the issue is so important. My answer: I believe compassion requires the abandonment of the belief in free will.

Albert Einstein did not believe in free will. In fact, he felt so strongly about it that he included this issue in the brief "Credo" he recorded before he left Germany for the last time in 1932. Einstein wrote that remembering that there is no free will "reconcile[s] me with the actions of others, even if they are rather painful to me. This awareness of the lack of free will keeps me from taking myself and my fellow men too seriously as acting and deciding individuals, and from losing my temper."[42]

To feel justified in assigning blame for an action or thought that we find objectionable we must believe that the action or thought is the product of free will: someone is intentionally or premeditatedly behaving in a wrongful manner. They are doing wrong *on purpose;* they *could* have behaved differently if they had wanted to. They *should* have known better. Similarly, the only way we can feel shame is if we feel we *could* have behaved differently than we did.

Imagine that someone rounds a corner and walks right into you, and you feel justified in blaming them for their inconsiderate carelessness: "Watch where the hell you're going!" You then notice that this thoughtless twerp is wearing dark glasses and carrying the white-tipped cane of the blind. Ouch! All justification for blame instantly vanishes and you find yourself asking the blind person's pardon. The dramatic shift in your attitude occurs because you can no longer convincingly perceive deliberate wrongdoing. This individual literally could not see you, thus did not *choose* to walk into you, and, therefore, was not to blame for carelessness, thoughtlessness, twerpiness, etc.

It is my contention that our subjective beliefs render each and every one of us as blind and as deserving of compassion as the "thoughtless twerp" in the above example.

If we believe in free will, then a person's actions or thoughts must be a perfect reflection of who that person is ("Ugly is as ugly does!"). If you do something stupid, then you *are* stupid. If I do something wrong, then I *am* wrong. If he does something evil, then he *is* evil. If she does something mean, then she *is* mean. If we believe in free will, then everyone is guilty...*by reason of free will.*

Lucky for us, free will is a lie.

❖

I think one of the reasons the belief in free will is so hard to budge is because we confuse will with free will.

"Will" [Webster's]: *the power of making a reasoned choice or decision, or of controlling one's own actions.*

Most people have had the experience of using willpower to restrain themselves: wanting to do something and choosing not to. Our brains have evolved a mechanism for reflective thought in the cerebral cortex that allows us to apply the brakes to our impulses. When we see a good-looking person on the sidewalk our "lower-brain" (in charge of instinctual behavior) sends a signal to have sex, and our cerebral cortex (usually) keeps us from jumping out of the car to act on the urge. It feels like we exercised restraint, and it doesn't feel like there was anything outside of us that caused the curbing of our impulse: we did it of our own volition.

However, this restraint is as lacking in free choice as the decision to wear clothing to work. We are hemmed in by all the rules of society that were programmed into our minds. We did exercise our will, but it's inaccurate to call it free.

Will isn't just about restraining impulses; it also involves positive action. Some years ago in a small town Arthur and I created a weekly television show on the local cable system. We came up with the concept, sold the cable company on the idea, went out into the community to find interesting stories to tell, and convinced businesses that it was a valuable form of advertising. We had a successful, popular program that ran for six years, which ended only because we decided to move. And it was created and sustained entirely by our will. No one was coercing us to create; we had no boss to report to; it relied entirely on our initiative. At any point it could have collapsed because it was solely dependent upon us having the will to get up every day and work.

Yet to call this an example of free will is a mistake. There were all kinds of constraints operating on us, including the need to earn a living. I would never have chosen television production for a career as a free will choice; I hate TV and almost never watch it. I got into video production in a very backwards manner. In the early 1990s Arthur and I had created some videos purely for pleasure and someone said to us, "Your work is really high-quality, why don't you make a nature video of this area for tourists to buy?" We did, and video production became a creative and rewarding way to earn a living.

Einstein wrote eloquently about the confusion of will and free will in a letter to a friend:

> Honestly I cannot understand what people mean when they talk about freedom of the human will. I have a feeling, for instance, that I 'will' something or other; but what relation this has with freedom I cannot understand at all. I feel that I will to light my pipe and I do it; but how

can I connect this up with the idea of freedom? What is behind the act of *willing* to light the pipe? Another act of willing? Schopenhauer once said, 'Man can do what he wills but he cannot will what he wills.' When you mention people who speak of such a thing as free will in nature it is difficult for me to find a suitable reply. The idea is, of course, preposterous.[43]

We all have the experience of making choices. If free will doesn't exist how do we make choices?

The human brain has evolved the amazing ability to perceive multiple possibilities in any situation. When I feel hunger I can consider various options: not eat because I'm on a diet, pull leftovers from the refrigerator, take a cookbook down off the shelf, order pizza delivered, get in the car and go to a restaurant, etc. When my cat feels hunger she just goes to her bowl or bugs me to fill it. She doesn't have the number of options that I do. Because our mind provides us with all these possible actions, and we act on one of them, we think that proves we have free will. All it proves is that we have an awesome analytical brain that can offer up multiple solutions to a single problem.

When making a choice the mind operates through a reasoning process, which could be described as a particular psychological and physiological configuration interacting with particular external stimuli. This formula simply means that if all the external and internal variables were known—all of the contributing factors including the exact configuration of the individual belief filtration system—we could predict with absolute certainty what we were about to choose (not that this level of knowledge is currently possible). We could then see that our choice was in fact a foregone conclusion and not an expression of free will at all.

Let's say I'm offered a choice of two flavors of ice cream (external stimuli), and I like both flavors more or less equally (my psychological-physiological configuration). Even though it appears that I am reasoning over which flavor to choose, I will inevitably pick one because, at the exact moment of choice, my psychological and physiological make-up (the memory of the taste, my mood at the moment, my body chemistry and blood pressure), interacting with external stimuli (the light in the room, the appearance of the ice cream selections in the case, the temperature of the air, the music playing in the background), will render that flavor most appealing. I do not freely choose; the countless existent variables conspire to make one flavor literally irresistible to me at the moment of choice. For example, I like chocolate-chocolate chip and butter-pecan equally. But, when I have had a bad day, or when I'm about to start my period, there is no substitute for chocolate. I would never pick butter-pecan on one of those days.

But if this is true how do we change?

I did a lot of cocaine at one point in my life. After a couple of years I decided I didn't like what the drug was doing to me and I went through a period of struggle trying to quit. If I don't have free will how did I stop taking cocaine?

Imagine a seesaw. On one side of the seesaw are stacked the positives or benefits of a behavior and on the other side are piled the negatives or harmful consequences. When I first started doing cocaine all I saw were the benefits: I felt gloriously high and free from inhibitions. I loved the feeling of my mind racing. I loved the sexual energy. My cocaine seesaw was buried in the ground on the positive side; there was nothing on the negative end.

As time went on, though, I began to notice negative aspects of cocaine use. For example, I would feel terrible when I started to come down. Evidence began to accumulate on the negative side of the seesaw, although this side was still outweighed by the positives. As I continued to use cocaine, more and more negative consequences manifested: cocaine was consuming my life, nothing else mattered, the crash at the end showed the artificiality of the high, the sense of freedom was really just a mirage, and sex was going to increasingly weird places.

The negative evidence built up until one night, lying in bed in a futile attempt to sleep and hating myself once again, I had the image of being perched on the edge of the event horizon—the point of no return—of a black hole. I was desperately resisting the pull of the vortex so as not to be sucked in and lost forever. This was a turning point for me. What happened was that the negatives had built up sufficiently that the seesaw, for the first time, tipped down on the negative side.

But this wasn't the end of my cocaine use. The negatives had accumulated enough mass to tip the scale, but they were still close in weight to the positives. As a consequence my seesaw began to bounce back and forth between positive and negative. This was my period of "struggle." I still saw positives in doing coke even though I was more and more convinced of the harmful aspects. During the period when I was trying to quit the negatives kept building up and the positives kept shrinking. One day the seesaw flipped for good and the negative side hit bottom. There was nothing left on the positive side and I never did cocaine again.

What happened was my a/e filtration system was altered through the learning process of experience. We are capable of modifying and even replacing the beliefs that make up our a/e filter, although it often takes extreme circumstances (like getting addicted to a drug) before we are willing to do so.

❖

Most of us love the idea of being in control, yet the irony is that in many areas of human endeavor mastery comes when we *relinquish* conscious control. This is true in art, music, and sports. When an athlete talks about being "in the zone," what they mean is reaching that place where they act and move without conscious thought or control: the sensation is of moving perfectly without any wasted motion or effort, following precisely the flow of here-and-now reality.

An artist, when asked about the source of their work, will often respond, "I don't know, it just flows through me." Gary Larson, for example, the creator of *The Far Side* cartoon series, was constantly asked to name the source of his wild ideas. I heard him respond to this question at a book signing by saying, "I don't know, I don't analyze it, and I don't want to analyze it, because if I did the flow might stop."

Musicians aren't thinking about the next note when they are playing. They feel the music move through them and it brings the next note with it in an endless flow.

Psychologists have developed a shorthand notation for the conscious and subconscious minds. Self 1 is the conscious mind (of course it has to be number one!). The subconscious mind is called Self 2. Tor Norretranders, in his book on consciousness, *The User Illusion*, describes the conflict between our two minds: "The problem is that Self 1 wants badly to control and decide everything. But it is Self 2 that carries out the performance as a tennis player or music maker. It is Self 2 that knows how to perform a good forehand, while Self 1 is concerned with how you look, how the next shot should be carried out, the result of the last forehand, etc." If we let Self 1 chatter away, we can be sure we'll miss the next shot.[44]

We have all experienced this conflict when we learned to drive a car. At first, our conscious mind was very much in control, and our movements were jerky and uncoordinated. As we gained experience, and the driving was more and more relegated to the realm of the subconscious, our movements smoothed out and driving the car was much more comfortable for us and our passengers.

Yet most of us ferociously cling to the belief that we have conscious control of our lives through free will.

9

The Wizard of Subjective Mind

"The only sin is self-hatred."
— *Das Energi,* Paul Williams [45]

Ironically, human beings cling to the belief in free will even though it is one of the principal sources of suffering in our lives. The crippling agony of self-hatred is given its teeth and its power solely through the belief that we have exercised free will and chosen every single "failure" and "wrongdoing" in our lives.

Insecurity. Shyness. Self-doubt. Regret. Guilt. Shame. Jealousy. Envy. Embarrassment. Everyone experiences these painful feelings at one time or another. All of us want to be strong and beautiful, fearless and true, and yet, whether we are consciously aware of it or not, all of us are encumbered by self-estimations of weakness, failure, ugliness, cowardice, and falsity. A human being is a house divided against its self. We are all locked in conflict with ourselves. We are all haunted by an inner accuser: a persistent critic who monitors, questions, and ruthlessly evaluates our every thought and deed. We are all crippled by this terrible mental affliction that truncates our experience of life.

When I was nine, I was invited to a slumber party at my next-door neighbor's house. She went to a Catholic school so I didn't know any of the other girls and was intimidated because they were all older than me. The next morning we all lined up to use the one bathroom. The line seemed to stretch in front of me forever as each girl took an interminable amount of time to complete her toilet. My bladder was bursting, but instead of "acting like a baby" and demanding access, I tried to be a "big girl" and hold it. I held it all right—until it was way too late. Realizing the dam was giving way I rushed into a nearby room, slammed the door, and pissed all over myself and the rug.

When my friend's mother found me, I was in a state of total mortification. My shame was so deep that it took thirty years before I could tell this story without experiencing some of the original agony. I blamed myself. I hated myself. I couldn't forgive myself. I was a defective, rug-pissing loser! When the day finally arrived that I could laugh about this experience, I knew I had overcome my shame. The key was facing the objective fact that I was an inexperienced nine-year-old child and could not help myself in that situation. I no longer saw pissing my pajamas as a glaring and immutable character defect. But you can be sure that for all those years before my laughter, this event had been part of the "loser" narrative of My Story. It was definitely part of the evidence that justified my self-hatred.

Self-hatred is a universal human problem. This eminently includes those "winners" who have somehow managed—usually through wealth, giftedness, or physical beauty (according to tribal standards)—to convince themselves and/or others that they are completely self-assured and free of all fear and self-loathing. We humans are perfectly capable of deluding ourselves that we are happy, and we can get legions of others to agree with us, but if we dig deep enough we will all discover a decidedly contrary opinion.

❖

We constructed our personality as a coping mechanism to deal with our staggering ignorance, as a way to fit in with our family and culture and play the game of life. We soon come to think of ourselves as this personality. And yet, deep within our subconscious, we cannot forget that we built this ego-structure, that we pre-date it, that we were there at its inception.

Our personality is a theatrical act we perform for the world. On the surface we identify with this act and live as though it is our true identity. But at some level we realize that we are more than this personality and that our ego-mask is simply a way of conforming to, and participating in, the world. This knowledge makes us insecure for life. We think of ourselves as phonies and pretenders—subject to all of the harsh condemnation that we think a faker deserves. Worse, we think that other people *aren't* faking it, that their personalities are truly who they are, and that we alone are bogus.

We spend our lives desperately projecting our "good sides" to ourselves and everyone else while attempting to conceal our "bad sides" from the same parties. The problem is that we are forever denied true peace and satisfaction because we are living a lie. We are faking a certainty that we do not possess.

Our subjective belief that we are flawed or imperfect is not an objective fact. What is an objective fact is that we were all born into a gigantic, mysterious universe and have created the best personality we could in order to survive in it. If we could let go of the blame and shame arising from our erroneous belief in free will, we could experience compassion for ourselves. As frightened and confused children, we literally did the best we could to figure out the optimum way to survive this thing called life, by playing the necessary games to the best of our ability. We put together the most effective survival act we were capable of, whether that act eventually resulted in Nobel Prize winner or serial killer.

Evolutionary biologists suggest that shame developed as a social control mechanism in the early period of human development when we were learning how to live in cooperative societies. If most people in a group shared their food with the others, but a couple of the members were selfish and kept their food to themselves, the group would suffer. Groups developed rules of behavior that included condemnation and ostracism for those who failed to cooperate.

When we break the rules of our social group, we experience a strong physical sensation, including the rushing of blood to the face. We hang our heads. These physical markers allowed others to know that we learned our lesson. This kind of shame is equivalent to physical pain: when I put my hand on a hot stove I feel physical pain that teaches me not to do that again. When I hide food from the others I feel emotional pain that teaches me not to do that again.

However, the subjective mind has twisted shame to mean much more, and as a consequence turned it into a destructive force.

Gay Talese wrote an interesting book about social mores entitled *Thy Neighbor's Wife*. He observed that the guilt we feel about breaking our culture's rules, such as smoking pot or cheating on our taxes, is used by rulers to keep us in check: "Who wants a nation of law-abiding citizens? What's there in that for anyone? ...Just pass the kind of laws that can neither be observed nor enforced nor objectively interpreted—and you create a nation of lawbreakers and then you cash in on guilt."[46]

Alan Watts made the same observation in *Beyond Theology*, "Clearly, the whole force of original, existential guilt is that it be an obscure and gnawing sense of being profoundly in the wrong, though for no discernible reason. Governments maintain this sense in a mild form by seeing to it that the laws are so complex that every citizen is inadvertently guilty of some crime, making it possible to convict anyone when convenient. Religions do it much more thoroughly, often suggesting that one's very existence is in some way an effrontery and an offense against God."[47]

Our subjective mind maintains control (that is, survives) in the same way:

Our subjective beliefs, assimilated in childhood, taken from our family and culture, create an ideal of normalcy in our subjective minds. We hold ourselves to this impossible standard of perfection (the "law" in the quotes above).

Our subjective mind records every failure to meet this standard, every wrong thing we have ever done, including the verdict that we *could* and *should* have not done it because we have free will. We judge ourselves imperfect and abnormal.

The subjective mind keeps us in line by constantly threatening to reveal to us the deeply suppressed case files of just how horrible, imperfect, and abnormal we really are. This is a survival tactic: by creating self-hatred and then exploiting our fear of facing it the subjective mind assures that we will never objectively question the accuracy of our subjective beliefs.

Just as a person who cheats on their income-tax walks and talks carefully where the government is concerned (lest they draw the government's attention and their tax-evasion be discovered), so do we remain terrified of and obedient to our subjective mind, never seriously challenging it lest our unspeakable shortcomings be thrust in our faces—and exposed to everyone else.

We dare not examine our subjective mind's case against us because we're convinced that to do so would require facing the ultimate horror: our self-hatred is fully justified. The courage to really confront our self-hatred, or even to acknowledge its existence, is well beyond most of us.

❖

If self-hatred isn't a symptom of insanity then what is? How balanced, functional, and rational can we be when our foundational belief is that the person staring back at us in the mirror is, to put it mildly, something less than satisfactory?

Physical self-mutilation, such as anorexia nervosa, is easily recognized as an expression of mental illness. The psychological self-mutilation of self-hatred, however, is so widespread and so politely overlooked that it is much more difficult to recognize. "Everyone has something about themselves they don't like" is accepted as a fact of life, and is considered largely harmless, and, like death and taxes, an inescapable part of being human. But when we stop denying not merely the reality but the actual scope of our self-hatred, this "harmless fact" is revealed to be a life-long nightmare resulting in a lifetime of self-diminishment. The self-mutilation arising from hating ourselves is as blindly destructive and life-robbing a mental illness as that of the anorexic who, imagining herself to be overweight, starves herself to death.

My husband Arthur, a talented singer-songwriter, observes that, "The reason artists are often discovered after their deaths is because they are no longer around to sabotage their careers."

Self-hatred lies like a black hole at the center of every human ego-identity and is sufficiently terrifying to guarantee that most of us will never approach it—much less objectively challenge it. We go through life putting the best face on things that we can, but we are never free of the terrible insecurities and regrets that are all produced by a titanic lie: that we should or could have acted differently than we did in any moment.

What are the implications of self-hatred? What does it mean to despise one's self, to find one's self unacceptable, to feel not as good as everyone else? What does it mean to look in the mirror and see something to be ashamed of, something to apologize for, something to hide, something that needs defending, something in perpetual need of improvement?

Self-hatred means a life of *dissatisfaction*, because if we truly believe that we are unacceptable then our lives must be unacceptable. How good, after all, could life ever be for those who hate themselves?

Life is good only in those rare moments when it happens to conform to our expectations of how it should be.

Self-hatred means a life of *deception*, of pretending to be something we're not. We're lifelong hypocrites. We deceive ourselves through denial—hiding our true self-opinion—and spend a lifetime trying to conceal what we consider to be our bad side from ourselves and everyone else.

Self-hatred means a life of *loneliness*, because real intimacy could expose our true ghastly nature. Self-hatred makes lasting love impossible. After all, who in his or her right mind could love someone like us?

Self-hatred means a life of *fear*, because we're always on the defensive lest someone find out the truth about us. The result is perpetual insecurity and anxiety.

Self-hatred means a life of *anger*, a chronic state of bitterness and resentment that our lives are flawed.

Self-hatred means a life of *envy*, we wish we were like those who appear not to be faking it (celebrities, for example).

Self-hatred means a life of *cowardice*, the unwillingness to speak our minds or stand up for what we believe in (what right does a loser have to act the hero?).

Self-hatred means a life of *justification*, the constant and hopeless struggle to prove ourselves worthy, a lifetime of hyper-competitiveness and over-achievement in order to compensate for, and distract ourselves and others from, our self-perceived inadequacy. The result is pride, arrogance, and lust for power and domination.

Self-hatred means a life of *pain* that we attempt to relieve with distractions and comforts such as food, possessions, TV, drugs, alcohol, sex, etc.

Self-hatred means a life of *shame*. We have a shadow side, a dark side that is reprehensible. We know what we did...or thought about doing...

No matter how positively we try to feel about ourselves, self-hatred, like an anchor, weighs us down and exhausts us with the effort to conceal it or break free of it. Self-hatred takes the edge off our happiness, our accomplishments, our loves, and our relationships. How, if our self-hatred is justified, could we possibly deserve anything good, true, or beautiful?

❖

In order to overcome self-hatred and love ourselves, much of modern psychology and new age thinking advises us to "embrace our dark side." Darkness implies evil. "Evil" or "sin," in the traditional use of the words, absolutely requires free will. We do not have free will. We don't have a dark side. We are physiological and psychological configurations interacting with external stimuli.

No dark side? Adolph Hitler had no dark side? Hitler attempted to conquer the world while committing mass murder on an unprecedented scale because his subjective belief system was massively distorted. He was extremely confused in his thinking. Even Hitler is innocent by reason of insanity. Even Hitler is deserving of compassion.

Evil: *believing in and/or acting upon a false belief. [A belief is false to the exact extent to which it fails to admit to its limitations.]*

Examine these two statements: 1. The universe is fourteen billion years old. 2. According to present scientific knowledge, the universe is approximately fourteen billion years old. What's the difference between them? The second statement is more objectively factual because it recognizes and acknowledges its limitations.

From mass murder to armed robbery to shoplifting to suicide bombing to insider trading to backbiting to the smallest act of cruelty, evil arises from a state of mental confusion that can drive the believer to commit the most beastly atrocities imaginable. "Evil-doers" believe, and act upon, false beliefs that justify their particular crimes and misdemeanors. Evil is what you think and/or do when you're crazy. These ideas will be investigated more thoroughly in the "Crime and Punishment" chapter.

❖

Subjective beliefs are always vulnerable to change by confrontation with objective facts. Our personality is a collection of surviving objective and subjective beliefs about who we are. A belief is susceptible to change/death by exposure to the truth, to reality. The best defense of a vulnerable belief is an offense: fiercely aggress against any objective questioning or examination.

I've noticed that I don't have a lot of attachment to the validity of my objective beliefs. When I find I'm wrong about something objective, I usually shrug my shoulders, say, "Oh," and update my mental files. For example, when we moved to a house with a steep driveway surrounded by trees, I didn't think I needed to rake the driveway. My belief was that the leaves would be crushed by the car's tires and wouldn't be a problem. The first winter we slipped and slid every time there was a little ice or snow. One day I realized the leaves were the culprit—the snow melted much faster on the gravel than on the leaves—and I have raked the drive ever since. No problem.

But I have a lot of attachment to my subjective beliefs. I think they are part of the essence of who I am. For example, I have been very attached to the subjective belief "I am a nice person." I conveniently ignored all the times I was rude to people who got in my way while driving, or the awful way I would often treat customer service representatives (or worse, telemarketers) on the phone. And every time I was angry and mean to Arthur it was really his fault of course—he had done something wrong and I was justified in whatever I did or said. I'm a nice person after all! My ready-to-hand rationalizations for my not-nice behavior ensured I would not question the truth of this subjective belief.

The human mind has a natural inclination towards truth and introspection. This is the function of the analysis/evaluation filter: to comprehend the world. But when we turn our objective analysis on ourselves, we threaten the survival of our subjective beliefs.

Our objective mind alone determines whether a subjective belief stays or goes. A thousand people can call us a drunk, legions can stand in line to warn us about our overindulgence and obvious dependency on alcohol, yet it is only when we objectively see for ourselves the falsity of our subjective belief, "I can handle drinking," that we are empowered to reject that belief and to come out from under its destructive domination. Only our objective mind has the power to challenge and change our unquestioned subjective assumptions about reality.

Our objective mind's introspection, however, is ferociously resisted by our subjective mind's defense system, because subjective mind has convinced us that it is who we really are and change/death of subjective mind means the death of us.

Self-hatred is the subjective mind's defense system.

We could liken self-hatred to an invisible deflector shield. This shield actively resists objective examination. This is its sole purpose. Self-hatred is a mechanistic reflex, nothing personal, just the business of form-survival. Self-hatred is how the subjective mind survives.

When we think about self-hatred we ordinarily think of that internal, interminable, infernal list of our self-determined shortcomings, wrongdoings, wrong thoughts, and general deficiencies. We avoid the subject of self-hatred like the plague because we are convinced of the legitimacy of these harsh subjective value judgments we've made about ourselves.

We avoid objective self-reflection because we're afraid of what new imperfections we might find lurking in the dungeons of our minds. We're already aware of plenty of our faults, so who wants to add to the list through self-examination?

Happily, it now appears that we have taken self-hatred far too seriously! Self-hatred is merely a mechanistic reflex generated by subjective mind in order to maintain its structural integrity. Subjective mind doesn't want to be questioned so it scares us away by convincing us that it has a fully documented catalogue of our faults, a dossier so terrible that we could not bear to face it. We are bullied and controlled for a lifetime by this blackmailer.

Our subjective mind protects itself like the wizard in *The Wizard of Oz*. It keeps all intruders at bay by a formidable and threatening display of fire, smoke, and mirrors: "I am the great OZ! Approach me at your peril! Grovel before my power and awesomeness, you weak and sniveling nothings!" But when we face the Wizard down, when our objective mind (reduced by the enslavement of subjective mind to the size of a small lap dog) manages to pull back the curtain and expose the true nature of the wizard, we discover a little con-artist pulling levers to maintain a protective illusion of impenetrable strength.

At such a moment of clarity, the whole justification for our self-hatred is revealed to be entirely specious, a smoke and mirrors subterfuge designed to conceal the truth. We don't have free will, we are confused about reality, and we have always done the best we were capable of. We are innocent by reason of insanity. All of this is there to experience...once we've faced the wizard down.

10

The Pacifier of Pride

"Atticus Finch was the deadest shot in Macombe County in his
time," Miss Maudie said.
"Looks like he'd be proud of it," I said.
"People in their right minds never take pride in their talents," said
Miss Maudie.
—*To Kill A Mockingbird*, Harper Lee [48]

Another offshoot of the belief in free will is pride. The subjective
mind doesn't just use the threatening stick of shame and self-hatred
to control us. It also dangles a tempting carrot: if we have free will,
after all, surely we are entitled to take credit for our good behavior,
our accomplishments, our talents, our right choices.

Taking pride in our accomplishments seems perfectly harmless,
just, and even desirable. So why was pride considered the worst of the
Seven Deadly Sins by the medieval Catholic Church? What is pride?

"Pride" [Webster's]:

*1. a high or inordinate opinion of one's own dignity, importance,
merit, or superiority, whether as cherished in the mind or as displayed
in bearing, conduct, etc.*

*2. a becoming or dignified sense of what is due to oneself or one's
position or character; self-respect; self-esteem.*

*3. pleasure or satisfaction taken in something done by or
belonging to oneself; believed to reflect credit upon oneself.*

What is interesting about these definitions is their proprietary
nature. Pride, it seems, is something due to us because of *our* talents,
our gifts, *our* possessions, *our* actions, *our* character, and *our*
position. We feel pride is justified because we believe that we have
willfully and deliberately—that is freely—chosen our talents, gifts,
possessions, actions, character, position, etc. And because we have

freely chosen them, we are responsible for their existence and are therefore entitled to take pride in them.

I breezed through school with high grades and graduated from Northwestern University with a bachelor's degree in Molecular Biology and Biochemistry with a B+ average. If I hadn't enjoyed marijuana and sex so much it would have been higher. As I said in the My Story chapter my intelligence was a source of pride to me from an early age and a way for me to feel superior to others.

But, when I look more closely, what was the true source of my intelligence? If I'm honest, I can see that it is a gift that I really had nothing to do with. My intelligence was given to me in the same way as my curly hair. Aside from the genetics, what responsibility could I claim for being born to educated, intelligent parents, being raised in an intellectual atmosphere that encouraged the use of the mind (reading books instead of watching TV), in a family structure that made sure I did my homework, and in an economically privileged social class that supported a great school system? All of these factors helped me sail through school with high grades. The truth is my pride at being smart is actually an expression of arrogance: I think (I hope) my intelligence makes me better than other people. Only by claiming that I am responsible for my intelligence can I use it to feel superior.

Some readers may protest, "but what about my hard work? Surely I deserve credit for the results of my efforts?" I'll use the example of the TV show Arthur and I created. I worked very hard to make that a success. And yet I don't take credit for it. I worked hard because: the only way to make it work was to cover all the tasks ourselves—the small town wouldn't ever provide enough income to allow us to hire employees; I have a very high standard of excellence (part of my psychological make-up) and worked much harder than many people would have thought necessary; my intelligence made the technical aspects of the production, which would have presented insurmountable obstacles to others, relatively easy; I'd been self-employed for a number of years already so I understood some of the difficulties involved; the lessons in humility and compassion I had learned from working on the philosophy in this book made me treat all the people of the town, from eminent scientists to simple country farmers, with equal respect and interest. I could go on...but my point is that I don't take credit for my success. Rather, I am conscious of and thankful for all of these components that, combined, brought about a positive result.

The third dictionary definition of "pride" talks about pleasure and satisfaction in a job well done. This feeling of fulfillment is wonderful; it only becomes a problem with the second half of that definition, "reflecting credit on oneself." It is possible to enjoy the fruits of our hard work, the achievement of a goal, or the creation of a work of art without it *meaning* something about us.

Being allowed to take credit for our gifts and accomplishments helps soothe the pain of our self-hatred. We're all encumbered with shame and guilt, but we hide these feelings beneath our gifts and accomplishments. We try to convince ourselves, and everyone else, that our self-hatred doesn't exist by a dazzling and hopefully distracting display of our good sides.

Consider this: *If you don't take the credit, you don't have to take the blame.*

Conversely, if you *do* take the credit, you absolutely *must* take the blame. You can't have one without the other.

Taking credit is all about making us feel better about ourselves: a reassuring pat on the back that says "I'm okay." The problem is that our subjective mind is not content to be just plain okay; it desperately needs to feel at least better—and preferably *best*. The need to be best is understandably driven by the need to overcome the self-hatred that makes us believe that we are the *worst*. Taking credit allows us to feel superior, even if this is not conscious, and puts us in competition with everyone else.

Taking credit is, in reality, arrogance. The Latin root of the word "arrogance" means *to claim for oneself*. This is why the medieval Catholic Church considered pride the greatest sin: pride meant taking the credit away from God.

Pride says, "I did it all by myself," blind to the obvious fact that no one stands alone. As the saying goes, all of us stand on the shoulders of our ancestors. The brilliant inventor who creates a revolutionary device working alone in his basement laboratory is still building on the achievements of past inventors and scientists.

An old folk-saying admonishes: "'My, look at the dust we raise,' said the ants on the chariot wheel."

Carl Sagan once remarked that in order to truly make an apple pie from scratch one would have to first bring the universe into being.[49]

❖

Pride is about standing out.

Perhaps the most terrifying concept to most people is the idea of their insignificance, of not being a noteworthy individual. Significance is equated with survival because it promises a form of immortality. Insignificance suggests that we are of such little consequence that, after a lifetime of being ignored, no one in the future will ever know (much less care) that we existed!

The Total Perspective Vortex, the ultimate torture machine in Douglas Adams' *The Hitchhiker's Guide to the Galaxy,* forced one to experience the size of one's body relative to the dimensions of the entire universe. The resulting feeling of crushing insignificance reduced the victim to a permanent vegetable state.[50]

When I was a teenager I wanted to be like Jesus (that is, like the Jesus as taught in my Sunday school class). I wanted to live a life of love and peace like Jesus did. Later I realized that I also envied Jesus for being someone who was so remarkable that he was being talked about two thousand years after his death. I wanted people to be talking about me that way! Which did I really want, love and enlightenment or immortal fame? In our culture it looks like fame is a surer path to significance and immortality than love and enlightenment.

❖

Shame and pride counterbalance one another. Shame and pride are used by subjective mind to block any attempt to truly know our self. To know our self we have to question who we really are. Under the spell of our shame, we're too afraid to question. Under the spell of our pride, we're too satisfied to question.

How many celebrities have demonstrated an incredibly self-destructive side to their personalities? The more rich and famous some people become the more their ego swells; they are given a lot of agreement that they should feel proud. But this inflated sense of self-worth must co-exist with the pre-existing sense of guilt and shame common to us all. The more the external praise is piled on, the greater the conflict with the inescapable internal demerit list. The greater the honor, the more painful the self-hatred becomes. "What if they find out the truth about me? Then they won't think I'm so great! They must really be stupid not to see my flaws." The self-destructive behavior of the rich, famous, and gifted is the way many of these people unconsciously cope with this conflict.

Our self-image is analogous to the classic story of *The Beauty and the Beast*. The subjective mind, in the process of defining our self-image, creates two selves: a beauty and a beast. The beast is our bad side: all of our self-perceived faults, shortcomings, and deficiencies (the justification for our self-hatred). The beauty is our good side: all of our accomplishments, talents, and positive attributes (the justification for our pride). Life becomes an endless battle between self-hatred and pride, with all of us believing that happiness lies in a final victory of beauty over beast. This is an illusory dream. The truth is that the beauty cannot exist without the beast. Beauty and beast are two sides of the same coin and cannot be separated.

In depictions of *The Beauty and the Beast*, beauty seems to always be a woman, and the beast a man. For a long time I believed in this myth and brought it into my relationships: Arthur (male hog) was all beast and I (female princess) was all beauty. This resulted in a terrible state of inequality between us that killed our love.

My Story of my relationship with Arthur has been that I'm even-tempered and fair-minded, while Arthur is an emotional roller coaster. When we argued, I would believe that I was being rational and trying to resolve the issue, while Arthur was alternately sulking or frothing with rage. In recent years I have discovered that my sweet and kind act is how I exert power and control in the relationship. I pretended to accept things that really bothered me, and I managed to convince myself that these things didn't matter (when they did)—and this cowardly behavior was supposed to demonstrate how sugary-sweet I am! The way I exerted control was by playing it nice, combined with being weak. A weakling surrenders superficially, but seethes with resentment.

I wouldn't stand up to Arthur's bully act. Instead I would try to look perfect and blameless to contrast with his "beastly" behavior. Making the beast feel guilty is a powerful weapon. I was not acting from love or niceness; I was out to get my way by whatever means necessary.

My realization that I too have a beast side has been of great benefit to our relationship. The truth is Arthur and I are equally beauty and beast. It is only in that equality that we can find love.

How does the traditional story of *The Beauty and the Beast* end? Beauty no longer sees the Beast as a monster—Beauty sees the Beast as beautiful. But Beauty stays the same—she's all beauty, all the time. The film *Shrek* updated the classic fairy tale. Shrek was an ogre; he fell in love with a beautiful princess named Fiona. During the course of the film Fiona comes to love Shrek because of his gentle and kind nature. Finally it is revealed that she is actually an ogre just like Shrek. The movie ends with the lovers being *equally* Beauty and Beast.

The beauty self-image created by subjective mind is not true beauty; it is in fact an imitation of beauty, a pseudo-beauty. Pseudo-beauty is only capable of delivering pseudo-satisfaction.

Pseudo-beauty requires constant effort and vigilance in order to keep the beast concealed (from ourselves as well as others). This is why so many of us try to act as though we are perfect and are so reluctant to admit to any serious fault. This is why we are fiercely competitive. This is why it is so hard for us to change.

Because we mistakenly believe happiness lies in the victory of Beauty over Beast we continuously strive to prove ourselves worthy. We must work tirelessly to promote our positive attributes because there is always shame and guilt gnawing away at our consciousness and reminding us of our inner beastliness. We are always uncertain and on the defensive lest our beast, like an uncouth relative, show up at our elegant soiree and spoil everything by pissing in the punch bowl and lighting farts on the candles.

Happiness lies not in the victory of beauty over beast, but in transcending the self-image of beauty and beast and their never-ending struggle. Happiness, love, and satisfaction, as we shall see, can be experienced only when we accept what is. Happiness arises from accepting ourselves exactly as we are right now.

True goodness, like true beauty and true happiness, lies in a realm beyond the beauty-beast dichotomy, beyond the realm of the subjective mind.

True beauty is selfless, compassionate, caring, appreciative, generous, open, humble, free of artifice, aware of its limitations, non-judgmental, non-competitive, accepting. True beauty requires no effort because it has nothing to conceal and nothing to promote. True beauty is an expression of ourselves as we are, with nothing hidden and nothing to apologize for.

11

Crime and Punishment

When I've talked with people about free will, the subject of crime often comes up. The thinking goes something like this: If we're not to blame for our actions, or we don't have shame to keep us from misbehaving, then we can and will do anything we want with total impunity, which would lead straight to anarchy. Only guilt and shame, along with legal (and, for some, divine) retribution prevent us from running wild in the streets, committing every crime possible. Nice opinion we have of ourselves.

How does a philosophy of universal human insanity answer these concerns?

A crime is always justified in the mind of the perpetrator. A person's particular psychological and physiological configuration, interacting with particular external stimuli, makes their actions totally justified within their individual reality. No matter what the crime, from stealing to murder to jaywalking, their mind-generated reality says, "This is the best way for me to behave in order to survive."

Our subjective mind allows us to make endless excuses for our behavior. Stealing is justified by such beliefs as, "It isn't fair that others have nice things when I don't, so it's okay to shoplift." How about this classic: "The government wastes money by the ship-load anyway, so what's the big deal if I fudge a bit on my taxes?" And, the motorist's favorite: "Everyone else was driving eighty, officer, I was just keeping up with the flow of traffic!"

Dr. James Gilligan, a psychiatrist who directed the Center for the Study of Violence at Harvard Medical School and was in charge of psychiatric services for the Massachusetts state prison system for ten years, begins his book on violence with this message: "The first lesson...is that *all violence is an attempt to reach justice*, or what the violent person perceives as justice, for himself or for whomever it is on whose behalf he is being violent...Thus, *the attempt to achieve and maintain justice, or to undo or prevent injustice, is the one and only universal cause of violence.*" [italics in the original][51]

In other words, no matter how horrible an act of violence might be, the perpetrator believed he or she was doing the right thing— that's how delusional a human can be.

The Nazi death camps are among the most horrific acts of violence humans have committed in our history, what we now call "crimes against humanity." But looked at through the lens of Dr. Gilligan's understanding, those camps are another example of delusional insanity.

Adolf Hitler believed he was acting in his country's best interest. He believed he was restoring justice to Germany for the wrongs imposed after World War I, and that he was creating a better homeland for his countrymen. He believed, as did many others all around the globe at that time (including many in this country), that certain racial types, including Jews, were corrupting the purity of the white race. Clearly there were a lot of Germans who agreed with him. He was wrong, of course, but that doesn't change the fact that in his deranged mind-generated reality he thought he was right. Adolf Hitler was not evil, he was insane.

Riccardo Orizio interviewed former dictators, including Idi Amin of Uganda and Jean-Claude "Baby Doc" Duvalier of Haiti, for his book *Talk of the Devil: Encounters With Seven Dictators*. Orizio shows that each of the dictators believed that what they did—stealing their country's wealth, torturing and murdering political opponents, ruthlessly controlling their citizen's lives—was for the good of their country. These men and women believed that they were patriots saving their country from chaos or domination by another country.

Mr. Orizio quotes Baby Doc, at his exiled home in France, saying, "I'm very proud of my name. I'm proud of what my father and I did for Haiti. Under us the country was prosperous...I am still the only one who can save the country, which is now reduced to such a miserable state...I cannot remain indifferent to the misery of my people. As president I did a great deal for Haiti."[52]

Baby Doc is not evil; he is delusional.

Our criminal justice system is entirely based upon the belief in free will. One of the first considerations in a trial is whether or not the accused is sane. The legal definition of "sanity" boils down to "knowing the difference between right and wrong." When a person is found to be guilty, the thinking process for that decision goes like this:

(a) You know the difference between right and wrong.
(b) You have the power to freely choose between right and wrong.
(c) You willfully chose wrong.
(d) You deserve to be punished.

At serial killer/necrophile/cannibal Jeffrey Dahmer's trial in Milwaukee, one of the prosecution's arguments that the defendant was in his "right mind"—sane, aware of the difference between right and wrong, capable of rational choice, possessing free will—was that Mr. Dahmer had demonstrated prudent and rational thinking by using a condom when having sex with the corpses of his victims.[53]

Our society's primitive thirst for revenge is perfectly reflected in our criminal justice system. The need to punish law-breakers is so extreme that even unquestionably sick people like Jeffrey Dahmer are considered to be in full control of their actions. What other possible justification could there be for the assertion that Mr. Dahmer's use of a condom proved he was sane?

According to the philosophy presented in this book, Jeffrey Dahmer could not remotely help being a cadaver-raping, corpse-eating serial killer. Mr. Dahmer did not, one sunny day, freely decide to go out and start murdering young men so he could share his apartment with their putrefying corpses. His actions were motivated by the deepest mental illness, by compulsions totally beyond his control.

What does it say about a society that holds such obviously demented behavior to be the actions of a sane person?

The Dalai Lama gives us an insight into another way of perceiving someone who kills:

> I'm against the death penalty. Whenever I see photographs
> of convicted prisoners who are condemned to death row, I
> feel very disturbed and uncomfortable. You see, basically I
> think that everybody has afflictive emotions; the potential

for hatred or forceful anger is there within all of us. Because of the circumstances, something happened to these poor people and they acted on those emotions, but I think they have the potential for good in them as well.[54]

Can you, reader, acknowledge some compulsive behavior or thought pattern that is beyond your control?

How about that extremely common human failing called gossip? Almost everyone practices it, and almost everyone knows that it is unethical. The essence of gossip is cowardice: saying unkind things about another that we would not have the courage to say in their presence. We all know that talking behind someone's back is deceitful, yet when a juicy bit of gossip comes into our possession many of us seem powerless to keep it to ourselves and trade our code of integrity for the momentary thrill of blabbing the delectable details to the first willing pair of ears we can find.

I'm not much of a gossiper, in fact I'm good at keeping secrets— and one of the benefits of keeping your mouth shut is you hear more secrets! But I do have a compulsion in a similar vein: I love it when I see someone fail at an endeavor. My self-image is that of a loser and I'm extremely competitive, and when you put those two together the best way for me to win is for other people to lose. When I see someone fail in business, particularly one that is in any way in competition with mine, I gloat. When I hear that a couple is divorcing, I exult in my superior long-term relationship. And I have an overpowering urge to tell someone, usually Arthur, about the other person's trouble. Arthur would often look strangely at me when I did this, wondering why I was so excited about something that had such little impact on my life and such a negative impact on another's. But it was a compulsion—I couldn't stop myself when the opportunity arose.

Then one day in a Chinese restaurant my fortune cookie had exactly the message I needed to hear: "Don't delight in another's misfortune." I tucked that slip of paper in my wallet where I would see it regularly and it has helped me remember not to follow that particular compulsive line of thought any more.

What about compulsive eating? How many of us have experienced unconsciously eating an entire bag of chips while watching TV, or robotically eating a stack of cookies after a stressful day at work, barely tasting the food as we shovel in another mouthful?

Our body would never choose to have ten or twenty or fifty pounds of totally extraneous body fat sagging down its skeletal frame and exhausting its heart. Yet our subjective mind, with its ability to distort reality, justifies everything and allows us to ignore the bulging reflection in the mirror. At the extreme end of the spectrum, we can even ignore a freezer packed with human flesh.

Every honest person will admit to the existence of some habit, some compulsion, some desire—whether actualized in deed or not—over which they have no control. These weaknesses are usually a source of shame and are withheld from public view. Anyone who says they are not at the mercy of some demanding belief system is either lying or kidding themselves (see: delusional). If our compulsion is illegal, and in many cases it is, then we could, if caught, be subjected to the same ruthless code of "justice" we impose on pathetic wretches like Jeffrey Dahmer. Even if we're not caught, even if we don't indulge in our fantasies, our ruthless subjective mind faithfully notates our shortcomings in a shameful case for self-hatred that we can never escape.

Let me state for the record that anyone who thinks I'm expressing more sympathy for the deranged criminal than for the victims of their derangement is not getting the message. The likely reason for this is that they are unwilling to examine their own beliefs, and because they find abhorrent the idea that victimizer and victim are entitled to *equal* compassion.

Most of us will never have our private little vices, compulsions, fantasies, or crimes found out. We will never be on the receiving end of our criminal justice system. However, our *internal* justice system, that judge, jury, and executioner of subjective mind, is every bit as ruthless and compassionless as our external system. In fact, our external system of justice is simply a manifestation of our collective internal systems. Worse, our internal judge doesn't let us get away with a single thing. Like some peoples' idea of an all-seeing God (or children's idea of Santa Claus), it knows and sees everything we do. To paraphrase Jesus in the Sermon on the Mount: as we judge others, so are we judged...by the fixed standards of our own subjective mind.

Mercifully, few of us will ever experience a true urge to commit murder, much less a homicidal urge that we are incapable of resisting. A serial killer is driven by precisely such a compulsion, one so terrible and relentless in its demands that, once the cycle of murder begins, the only fear is having the ability to continue killing taken away: i.e., being caught. All seemingly sane behavior—craftiness, premeditation, stealth, eluding detection and arrest—is simply the ruling compulsion attempting to maintain its structural integrity. This includes the demented precaution of wearing a condom while having sex with a deceased victim. After all, why get sick and die when there are countless future victims to experience the thrill with?

We are so desperate to blame and punish criminals that we stretch the meaning of sanity to the point that it becomes meaningless—and expose our own insanity in the process. If someone is found to be legally insane, they are judged to be "innocent by reason of insanity" and committed to a mental hospital. The insanity defense enrages those who believe in free will because it appears the perpetrator is getting away with their crime. We bend over backward to prove the defendant's ability to be responsible for their actions, which opens the way for us to get at them with our punitive criminal justice system. The ancient code of an eye for an eye, the infliction of retributive pain, is what passes for criminal correction in twenty-first century America. This is madness and it does little if anything to deter crime.

The "moment of passion" is often used as an insanity defense: husband catches wife in bed with another man, kills both in a jealous rage, the jury is sympathetic, and the killer serves little or no jail time. First-degree murder, on the other hand, means malice aforethought—the crime was premeditated—and we throw the book or the death chamber at these people.

But it seems to me that the desire to harm another can only come from an insane mind. To have the desire to kill, or to cheat, or to destroy is clear evidence that a person is not in their right mind. The mafia hit man who kills for profit, the woman who slowly poisons her husband for the insurance money, or the kidnapper or terrorist who painstakingly plans the job months ahead of time is, I believe, actually *more* insane than the individual who kills in a moment of sudden passion! The premeditating criminals exhibit a chronic state of dementia: they are able to consciously live with their crime-in-progress over an extended period, to plan well ahead of the actual execution of it.

John Hinckley attempted to assassinate President Ronald Reagan in 1981. At his trial Hinckley was found to be innocent by reason of insanity and sentenced to a mental institution. Many people found this hard to swallow because Hinckley was clearly responsible for the shooting; he'd been tackled on the spot seconds after he'd fired his gun. As a result some states instituted a new plea, "guilty but mentally ill."[55]

In other words, this person *did* commit the crime, but his or her responsibility is muted by the mental illness.

But if it's true that we are all insane, then the cause of all crime, like all dysfunctional subjective-mind-driven behavior, is delusional thinking. All criminals are mentally ill.

I'm not advocating that serial killers or other dangerous criminals be allowed to roam free. But our prisons are bursting at the seams, which proves that our antiquated system of punishment isn't working. When we see crime as the psychological illness that it is, we will treat it accordingly: humane incarceration in the equivalent of a secured mental hospital with true rehabilitation and care. In addition, we could study these people and learn how to help others before they commit similar crimes. This as opposed to the human zoos of today's prison system: a hideous, dangerous, and humiliating experience that only brutalizes and further hardens the offender—before he or she is returned to our midst!

Our prisons are overflowing partly because of the so-called war on drugs. Psychotropic drugs (marijuana, hashish, mescaline, peyote, LSD, and psilocybin) have been particularly targeted in this "war" for a very telling reason: these drugs can lead to objective introspection and serious questioning of established beliefs—anathema to the subjective mind. Alcohol is a subjective-mind reinforcer—there's no one more sure of themselves than a drunk—thus is perfectly legal in most societies.

I'll touch on capital punishment only to say that every time a convicted killer is put to death every citizen in that society shares in the collective murder of an insane person. Capital punishment is a contradiction of everything the word "civilized" means; it is complete madness.

Society is, of course, collectively innocent by reason of insanity.

❖

Years ago I read an editorial by Tom Teepen, editorial page editor of the *Atlanta Constitution*, which examined the parallel cases of a just-convicted murderer and a goat named Snowball, who had recently butted his owner to death. The goat was about to be executed for his crime, but when it was revealed that the fatal butting had happened only after a long history of abuse by his owner, an outpouring of public sympathy ensued. The result was that Snowball was pardoned for his action and sent to a petting zoo (!).

Mr. Teepen compared Snowball's story to the case of the human accused of murder, a man who had a long history of cruel abuse when he was a child. No one seemed to think that this abuse should be a mitigating factor in his sentencing, and there was no outpouring of sympathy to save him from death row. The columnist's question: how could we have empathy for a goat, and none for a human being?[56]

The answer, of course, is that we believe that the human should have known better; he was fully able to choose right over wrong. The human, after all, has free will, while the poor dumb goat has none.

In the future people will look back compassionately on our primitive and barbaric judicial system, just as we look back with compassion on the beastly treatment of mental patients in nineteenth-century insane asylums.

12

Value

"There is nothing either good or bad, but thinking makes it so."
"Hamlet," Act 2 Scene 2, Shakespeare

In the last four chapters we have looked at the myriad negative consequences of the belief in free will. We'll now turn to another destructive subjective belief: relative value.

As we saw, our analysis/evaluation filter assesses value: better, worse, good, bad, pretty, ugly, etc. To "judge value" clearly assumes that value is relative; that value varies in quantity from spot to spot, from person to person; that there exists some range of value from crowning peak of ultimate perfection to utmost depth of grossest imperfection.

What is value?

"Value" [Webster's]: *the relative worth or importance of something or someone; whatever is desirable or useful.*

As this definition reveals, value has two distinct meanings. The first describes value as worth. "Worth" means the inherent character or substance of a person or thing. This is usually the meaning of the word "value" in the phrase "value judgment": we're assessing someone's or something's worth or merit as a person or thing.

The second meaning in the "value" definition ascribes utilitarian usefulness to value. When I want to drive a nail into the wall, a hammer is of more utilitarian value to me than a screwdriver. This does not mean that the hammer has more inherent worth than the screwdriver; it only means that, for this job, the hammer is more useful.

The definition also uses the word "relative," implying that variability is a central part of the meaning of value.

"Relative" [Webster's]: *existing or having its specific nature only by relation to something else; not absolute or independent.*

Is value relative? Does value vary from place to place, or from person to person?

To look closer at value we'll use the same razor as we did with reality. There are three categories of value. *Objective value* is concerned with utilitarian usefulness; *subjective value* is concerned with worth, and *actual value* is non-relative, absolute.

Just as the only reality is actual reality (subjective and objective realities are both mind-generated illusions), so the only value is actual value. Actual value is everywhere. *There is no place where value is not absolute.* Actual value is all there is. There is no variation or deviation possible in actual value. Actual value is non-relative.

Is there less value on Mars than on Earth? By what standard? Because Mars can't support life as we know it? That is a utilitarian assessment (Mars cannot support human life) distorted by a subjective judgment of worth (life-supporting worlds are better than non-life-supporting).

Is there more value in childhood than in old age? According to what measure? Where is the proof that the energy of youth is superior to the wisdom that (usually) comes with age?

Does joy have more value than agony? As the ancient *Tao te Ching* observes, you literally can't have pleasure without pain, up without down, left without right, old without young, life without death. Therefore joy and agony, youth and age, life and death, are imbued with perfect and equal value. Everything has equal value because everything is of equal importance in the flawless expression of a dualistic universe.

The universe is perfect; whole and complete; unvarying in value. Nothing is more or less worthy than anything else.

I once heard this joke about value: The major organs of the body had an argument about which is most important. The brain and the heart and the lungs and other organs went round and round about who is the greatest. But the asshole just shut up!

Actual value is the fundamental nature of reality. Actual value is in everything, but we humans seem to spend the majority of our lives complaining about its absence. That's because we're insane. We're living in a perfect universe but we can't see the perfection.

The apparent absence of value is another clue that our perception of reality is distorted.

❖

The demands of survival prompted the evolution of value judgment: if everything were perceived to be of equal value our minds would be overwhelmed by sensory input, resulting in mental chaos. Without the ability to select and prioritize incoming sensory data we would be incapable of functioning. As you recall, if the red leaves by the side of the road were as important as the red stop light ahead we'd never make it through the day alive. We *must* prioritize. Objective value-assessment, using the utilitarian standard of value, literally makes life livable.

All form is obsessed with objective value-assessment because objective value-assessment and survival are one and the same. The only value a surviving form recognizes is survival. In order to maintain structural integrity a form must constantly assess every thing and every situation as either pro-survival or anti-survival. The more something is perceived to be pro-survival the higher the objective value-assessment. The more something is perceived to be anti-survival the lower the objective value-assessment.

Until human beings evolved, all value-assessment was utilitarian.

When lions move too close to a zebra herd, the zebras will feel the utilitarian-value of their environment diminishing, and when that value is assessed as sufficiently low the herd will move away from the predators. Failure to do so will invite the ultra-low-value experience of being killed and eaten—low, that is, to the zebra, but deliciously high on the lions' scale.

The Three Little Pigs objectively value-assessed all available building materials and the pig that chose bricks survived because his value-assessment proved to be the most accurate. Had they lived in earthquake-prone country instead of a land plagued by the Big Bad Wolf, the sticks or straw materials would have been the most pro-survival/utilitarian choice.

❖

Utilitarian value-assessment is a critical evaluation and prioritization process based solely upon the criteria of survival-enhancing usefulness. Objective value-assessment says: when it's raining, seek shelter.

Subjective value judgment is all about *meaning* and *merit*. Subjective value judgment says: when it's raining everything is ugly and gloomy, sunny days are better.

Subjective mind imposes its notion of relative worth, significance, merit, morality, and aesthetics on top of the clean utilitarian framework of objective value-assessment. In our lions and zebras example, the zebras moved away from the lions simply because the environment was perceived to be of low utilitarian value: that is, it was clearly to the zebra's survival advantage to move away, but there was nothing inherently *wrong* with the lions. The lions are not low in worth because they are the zebra's predator. The attacking lions are not intrinsically "evil," or "bad," but human observers might subjectively value-judge it that way. In nature programs when lions attack the music becomes ominous and we think: "Oh look at that poor zebra being killed by that vicious lion!"

Objective value-assessment discerns the survival usefulness of a belief, behavior, or circumstance without questioning the inherent worth of the person or thing involved. Subjective value judgment, on the other hand, assumes that the usefulness of a belief, behavior, or circumstance is the literal indicator of the inherent worth of the person or thing involved.

This does not mean that objective value-assessment sees *actual value*; sees the perfection or absolute truth of what is. It just means that objective value-assessment doesn't question the intrinsic *worth* of what is. Again, a hammer is "more valuable" than a screwdriver when one wishes to drive in a nail, but only in terms of its usefulness for this particular task. Objective value-assessment selects a particular form (a hammer) as more appropriate than another form (a screwdriver) to realize one's purpose or task (driving in a nail). The intrinsic worth of any form is not called into question because objective value-assessment is only concerned with utility.

When selecting a tool for a job, objective value-assessment says, "This tool either works or it doesn't, and if it's not the right one I'll use another." Subjective value judgment cries, "Goddamned screwdriver doesn't work!" and hurls the "worthless piece of junk" through the window.

Subjective value judgment believes that worth is as relative as usefulness. If it works it is good. If it doesn't work it's bad and deserves blame. If I succeed I am right and a winner and should feel proud. If I fail I am wrong and a loser and should feel shame.

Subjective mind can distort our objective value-assessments to the extent that, unlike the zebras, we are capable of concluding that moving *towards* the lions is to our survival advantage! A masochist sees pain as pleasurable. An alcoholic rationalizes the guzzling of liquid poison. Nicotine addicts overlook the pain and trauma to their lungs caused by the inhalation of hot burning smoke. A suicide puts the barrel of a shotgun in his mouth totally convinced that this is the very best course available. Billions of people believe that the preservation of their tribe is worth risking the termination of the human race in a thermonuclear holocaust.

In order to survive unquestioned and unchanged, subjective value judgment poses as—thus is regularly confused with—objective utilitarian value-assessment. This confusion is highly detrimental to the performance of our objective value-assessments. We convince ourselves that we are acting from objective value-assessment when the truth is we're acting from subjective value judgment.

Objective value-assessment is not foolproof either. The lion-killed zebra may have found the grass a bit too tantalizing to move away from the approaching lions in time: an incorrect objective value-assessment which could be seen to strengthen the zebra line by removing a member who foolishly chose an extra mouthful of grass over personal safety. However, as usual, it is the subjective realm that causes us the most problems.

For many of us, when we fail at an endeavor we subjectively value-judge it to mean that there is something wrong with us, we aren't good enough to succeed, we're stupid, a loser, etc.

But in science there is no such thing as a failed experiment, that is, a worthless experiment. If an experiment doesn't produce the desired result, it still has worth by confirming that this particular path is not the way. Thomas Edison is said to have claimed, "I have not failed. I've just found 10,000 ways that won't work."

Someone submitted this nugget of wisdom to a "meaning of life" web page: "At the very least our lives may serve as a warning to others."

There is value in everything.

❖

Arthur and I have been together more than thirty years. Recently we had a conversation about our time in Florida, just a few years into our relationship, when we did a lot of drugs and engaged in some wild, reckless behavior. What was remarkable about this conversation was that we found ourselves remembering and describing this period as a time of out-of-control craziness (which it was). We'd both said similar things in the past, but this time our recollection was free of the usual defensiveness, shame, and denial that ordinarily distorted our memories.

My perspective was free of the usual subjective value judgments about what my behavior *meant*. I had believed I was a *bad* person because I did lots of drugs and had kinky sex. All of a sudden I saw I wasn't "bad," I was *innocent by reason of insanity*. I said, "I feel clean; it's like looking through a window that had been filthy and was just washed."

What allowed this experience to occur was that I had stopped denying that I was insane—and the result was I simply recalled my "out-of-control crazy" behavior the way I would recall any other memory. For the first time I attained something like true objectivity about this period of my life, and the clarity of the overview was incredible. I was free of the sting of embarrassment and guilt and the need to justify myself and rationalize my actions that I had always felt when remembering this time.

Thankfully, objective value-assessments are stored in memory separate from subjective value judgments. Otherwise we would never be able to recall an event from any other point-of-view than that of the affixed subjective value judgment. What happened to Arthur and I illustrates this. On the television show "Dragnet," Sgt. Friday used to ask for, "Just the facts." Arthur and I would never have been able to recall "just the facts," free of subjective value judgments, if those objective assessments had not been stored separately from the subjective value-added nonsense that followed.

When something traumatic happens to us, it's not the objective event that haunts us; it's what we subjectively value-judge the event to *mean*.

Psychologist Thomas Moore writes of his experience with a woman who introduced herself as an "incest survivor":

> In those opening words, she told me that she was identified with the story of incest…Without denying any of her pain and suffering, would she be able to see through her story of incest? Could she eventually become free to be an individual, rather than the main character in a story from her childhood? Had she accepted a cultural definition of incest as inevitable psychological trauma and so made it into her myth?"[57]

This woman believed that she was the person she was *because of* the incest; the incest *meant* that she was a victim who inevitably suffered.

Some years ago I realized that a major problem in my life was that I was always doing things "because of." I was angry because of…I was sad because of…I was happy because of…I was afraid because of…I was unhappy in my relationship because of…

I envied people who were single—single people live for themselves and do not have to change their behavior "because of" the person they live with. I envied rich people—rich people never had to do anything they didn't want to "because of" the need for money (my subjective beliefs in action).

I clearly believed that my life was at the effect of circumstances and people outside me. What I realized, through working on the ideas in this book, was that circumstances don't affect my happiness. My *attitude* about those circumstances is the only thing that matters. My happiness is dependent upon my attitude. My attitude is dependent upon my subjective value judgments.

I wrote a note to myself:

> I don't do anything because of you.
> I don't not-do anything because of you.
> I do everything I do because of me.

To me this sounds like the formula for an ideal life. The truth is we are always doing everything "because of" ourselves, anyway! We just use other people as excuses for why we are doing or not doing something.

I have used other people as crutches to get away with what I want to do but won't allow myself to experience wanting because it is "bad" or "immoral." For example, I used Arthur to get away with some wild sex that I have enjoyed but would never have allowed myself to experience on my own because I couldn't admit to myself that I wanted it.

Years ago on long car trips we would play sex games for hours, both of us excited by the idea that we might be seen by passing motorists (although only the ever-interested long-distance truckers could see down into the car). But at the same time I was ashamed of having these "dirty" desires, so I would say that I was doing it "because of" Arthur: it's his fault; he's the one who really wants to do it and I'm just going along with him; he's the one who is bad and immoral, not me. Not only was I lying to myself, I was cheating myself of some of the sexual pleasure: my shame blocked experience.

I am now on the lookout for "because ofs." I believe this is what it means to take responsibility for my life. I'm not responsible for what happens to me—I don't choose to get cancer or be mugged—but I can question my subjective value judgments of the events of my life, what getting cancer or being mugged *means*.

I think this is what Thomas Moore was trying to teach his "incest survivor" client: She did not choose to be victimized; she's not responsible for the incest occurring. But she *does* have the ability to objectively question her subjective beliefs about the event: the value judgments about herself and her attacker that she told herself are "because of" the incest. She can question what the incest *means*.

13

The Scale of Value

Our subjective mind is obsessed with worth and meaning. Our personality is formed and maintained by the attempt to establish our self-worth. In order to define our world and our self we subjectively value-judge everything. In the process, each of us creates an individual subjective "scale of value." Our estimation of our self, and everyone and everything else, is placed somewhere on this scale of perceived relative worth.

Objective value also has a scale, based upon critical judgment and utilitarian standards. A mountain climber's objective scale of value logically holds that falling off the mountain is "lacking in value" (anti-survival), while not falling off the mountain is "high in value" (pro-survival).

Our subjective scale of value is built from fixed subjective beliefs about positive and negative attributes of objective reality. As we've seen, reality is filtered through our individual subjective beliefs about right and wrong, good and bad, beautiful and ugly, cowardly and brave, noble and ignoble, decent and indecent. These beliefs create a rigid standard of value. No two human beings share identical subjective scales of value. From this point on, for the sake of brevity, the term "scale of value" will refer only to the subjective scale.

Our scale of value correlates with acceptability. If something is positive according to our scale, we find it acceptable. Conversely, if it's negative we find it unacceptable. The subjective mind has windows of acceptability defined by the positives on our scale of value. These windows of acceptability are what we call our personal taste.

My taste in paintings runs to 19th Century impressionists; Monet in particular. I think a lot of modern art is ugly and pointless and I find much of it unacceptable, while art from earlier centuries is beautiful and inspirational and acceptable. In my youth I thought my appreciation of the impressionists made me superior in my artistic tastes. Connoisseurs of modern art would undoubtedly find my taste in art ignorant.

As I've suggested, the ego-identity is like an onion, with layers that can be peeled off one by one. What we want to do is pull off the most destructive and insane layers first. Individual taste is the natural consequence of a unique subjective point-of-view and an invariably unique psychology and physiology. Individual taste makes for an interesting world of varied personalities. I'm not arguing for the elimination of personal taste.

However, there is a destructive byproduct of subjective value judgment: the erroneous belief that our tastes *mean* something, that our tastes make us superior to anyone who does not share them. What if we peeled off this layer of value, so that our taste was simply that, our taste, without it being a statement about our relative worth as a human being? We could have a splendid time enjoying the myriad expressions of individual perspectives by eliminating the competitive and negative aspect of our subjective mind that is always trying to make our taste superior to everyone else's.

Another destructive layer of the ego-identity onion is comprised of compulsive/obsessive behaviors, which pose as individual taste: drug addictions, eating disorders, hyper-sexuality, uncontrolled shopping, gambling, etc. We delude ourselves that our self-destructive appetites are simply the expression of an individual proclivity. In fact, these harmful compulsions and obsessions pose as benign individual tastes only in order to be left alone—the better to survive unchanged.

I have a taste for coffee. In fact, I consider myself somewhat of a connoisseur, and spend a lot of money on beans, filters, equipment, etc. I think this makes me superior to people who are content to drink supermarket brands of coffee. But the first time I tasted coffee I found it completely revolting. Once I got hooked on the caffeine kick my taste changed. Objectively, I can see that my taste for coffee is actually a caffeine addiction. All of my beliefs about being a connoisseur are just my subjective mind prettying up my enslavement to caffeine and allowing me to be proud of myself for being a gourmet! I'm like a junkie who boasts that she only shoots the finest heroin. All the nonsense about my refined taste for coffee is simply a way to justify my caffeine habit and give myself another way to feel superior.

Subjective mind has to be consistent in order to keep us convinced of its truthfulness (remember, this is how it survives). Once something is established as positive (or negative) on subjective mind's scale of value, whenever we cross paths with it in the world or inside ourselves, subjective mind *must* allow it to be experienced as acceptable (or unacceptable).

If we believe that cursing is "wrong," then we must negatively judge others when they curse, and we are bound to condemn ourselves when we curse. We never get away with the smallest infraction of our own rules, in spite of our subjective mind's masterful trick of allowing us to superficially delude ourselves that *our* transgressions are excusable (the soothing balm of rationalization).

We evade confronting our own negative self-estimation by value-judging everyone and everything else. Our default value judgment of others is shifted towards the negative end of the spectrum (in psychology, this is called the "negativity bias"). The root of this tendency is likely to be found in our primal animal awareness: "be on the lookout for danger" is obviously a pro-survival attitude. Flight/fight survival dynamics have programmed us to be more sensitive to the presence of negative stimuli than positive.

This heightened awareness of the negative was carried into the subjective realm, where the normal operating defense mode is to stand tall by chopping off everyone else's head. We feel better about our self-perceived deficiencies when we keep our attention focused on everyone else's. This is why soap operas and reality shows are so popular.

Another cognitive bias identified by psychologists is the "fundamental attribution error." When we observe others, we underestimate the influence of external factors on their behavior while overestimating the influence of internal factors. When it comes to our behavior, however, we do the exact opposite.

For example, if I carelessly drift over the center line of the road while driving, I will usually attribute my error to external factors: "I was distracted by the argument going on in the back seat," or, "this road is poorly designed." It certainly had nothing to do with *me*— I'm a good driver. But when I see another driver cross the center line, I attribute their action to internal factors: "she's a careless driver," or, simply, "what an asshole!" I always find extenuating circumstances and mitigating factors to excuse or lessen my mistakes while rarely extending the same courtesy to others.

The subjective mind has only one place for us on our scale of value: on top. The essence of subjective mind-dominated human interaction is competition. Childhood clichés say it all: "I'm the king of the hill!" "I got here first!" "My Dad can beat up your Dad!" "I know something you don't!" Subjective mind, freshly minted and ready for action, attempting to establish worth, prove superiority, maximize acceptability, rationalize any behavior to achieve its goals, and climb as high as possible in the pecking order of playground society. And a lifetime of this exhausting behavior stretching ahead...

The older we get, the more we learn to conceal these vicious displays of competitiveness. The only difference between a child's subjective mind and an adult's is that the child is far more blatant about putting others down in order to elevate him or herself. Society could not function if we remained as openly cruel towards one another as we were in the schoolyard. Even though we've learned to be more subtle (or covert) in expressing our value judgments, our social problems arise from the fact that we are still totally obsessed with being superior—that is, totally obsessed with being *right*. Remember, the survival strategy of the subjective mind is to convince us that our opinions are the truth—when you're right there's no need to change.

At the resort-town up-scale restaurant where I waitressed our patrons were mostly upper-middle-class lawyers, doctors, and stockbrokers who could afford second-homes on golf courses. A predominant assumption in our culture is that waiting tables is a low-class occupation, and this attitude is shared by customers and waiters alike. My fellow waiters and I would deal with our feelings of inferiority by verbally abusing obnoxious customers in the privacy of the kitchen. The swinging doors between the kitchen and the dining room defined two separate worlds. Out among the customers, we would smile and be obsequious, but in the safety of the kitchen we would viciously critique diners who were difficult or ridiculous. We would condemn their clothes, their lifestyles, their affectations, their political opinions, their relationships—anything and everything we could find to diminish them and elevate ourselves.

Since I was also the dining room manager I tried to find ways to help my fellow employees release stress. Once I found a large photograph of six hogs lined up at a trough (shot from the rear) and put it up in the kitchen with the title, "Table for Six." Another time I made an effigy of a customer for everyone to abuse as a form of therapy during one of our staff meetings. My fellow waiters and I gleefully poured hot coffee in the dummy's crotch, stabbed it with steak knives, and abused it with the worst epithets we could think of. I happily participated in this hate-fest in order to evade my own negative self-opinions (unfortunately, my scale of value held waiters to be inferior as well).

❖

Ordinarily our consciousness is dominated by negative subjective value judgments. Most of us find huge swaths of life unacceptable. And yet, once in awhile we cross paths with something so overwhelmingly acceptable to our individual scale of value that a great deal of our screen of awareness is suddenly cleared of negative value judgment. This is why we flock to natural spectacles like the Grand Canyon. We seek to be awed by an extraordinary experience of acceptability; we want to experience a positive feeling about life for a change.

The most dramatic example of the diminishment of negative value judgments is the experience we call "falling in love."

When we meet a person with an exceptional number of positive qualities (according to our scale of value), we are attracted to them; we find them extraordinarily acceptable. Whether over time or instantaneously, whenever a sufficient mass of acceptableness is experienced we find ourselves in love.

The phrase "falling in love" perfectly describes the out-of-control nature of the experience. When one is falling, one is totally at the mercy of the circumstances. Who would claim that one morning they made a free will decision to get up, get dressed, go out, and fall in love? We might take out ads in the personal columns, or frequent singles bars, but we have no idea where, when, or if the experience of love will occur. Falling in love is tantamount to a fluke shot in a game of pool: one's hand slips, and the cue ball banks three times around the table and manages to pocket the right ball.

Falling in love has been poetically described as the opening of the heart. Let's visualize the human heart as a bank vault. Its default position is closed and locked. To open the massive vault door you must enter the precise code of acceptability. This code alone triggers the delicate release mechanisms of the lock. When we meet someone with enough positive traits, the tumblers respond and the great protective door begins to open. All of this is a mechanistic inevitability, no different from Pavlov's famous salivating canines. When we see a person who matches our individual scale of acceptability we begin, figuratively (if not literally!), to drool.

The crucial point in the combination-lock analogy is that love is the open door experience, not the code that opens the door. The code of acceptability is made up of positives on an individual's subjective scale of value. These are fixed subjective beliefs about worth, *not* the love experience. These beliefs are positive value judgments, and though it is tempting to believe that they are the good kind of judgments, because they are value judgments they are still a subjective statement about the relative worth of an object.

In fact, a positive value judgment is simply the inevitable consequence of a negative value judgment. The negative value judgment "cursing is bad" automatically establishes the positive value judgment "not-cursing is good." In a dualistic universe, positive and negative are inextricably linked.

Value judgments are surviving thought-forms; mind-generated concepts.

Love is not a thought-form or concept. Love is experience.

I define "love" as: *the experience of unconditional acceptance of what is.*

When we experience love for another we see so many positives and so few negatives that we accept that person just as they are. The experience of love is extraordinary, because our ordinary experience of life is filled with negativity and non-acceptance.

When we experience love the seemingly all-powerful subjective mind is foiled by its own inflexible scale of value. The Achilles heel of subjective mind is its vulnerability to being rudely ejected from the command chair of consciousness by encountering someone with enough positive traits to generate the experience of acceptance.

Positive value judgments may be just as fixed and harmful as negative judgments, but when, like checks, they are presented at the bank's teller window, they must be found acceptable and cashed. We usually see these positive checks in very limited number (ordinarily being deluged with negative debits of condemnation and blame). When love happens, there is the equivalent of a run on the bank and the vault door swings wide open. Subjective mind is overwhelmed by the mass of positivity, to the point that, for a while, it is largely removed from the forefront of our screen of awareness.

Love transforms the lover. Not only is the object of our love acceptable to us, so is most of reality. It's actually a pleasure to wake up in the morning! And this ecstatic state is simply due to the fact that we are accepting reality to an appreciably greater degree than usual.

Friendship works the same way as love: the closer the friendship, the closer the alignment to each other's internalized scale of positive attributes. This is why like-minded people find and befriend one another. Friends have similar tastes and similar scales of value. There are exceptions where broad-minded individuals befriend someone with conflicting religious, political, and/or philosophical views, but in most cases there are enough other positive attributes satisfied on each friend's scale of value to permit the friendship to exist in spite of areas of conflict.

It is also important to note that like-minded people are the least likely to seriously challenge the structural integrity of one another's beliefs, an extremely desirable condition from the subjective mind's point-of-view.

One feature of scale-of-value-approved love is its sameness. Because we only fall in love when someone satisfies our list of positive traits, everyone we fall in love with will be very similar; they must conform to our same fixed list of positives.

As I mentioned earlier, soon after I met Arthur I was regularly struck by the similarities between Arthur and my college boyfriend. One night while Arthur and I were having sex, I looked into his face and he actually looked like my college lover!

Love is a very distinct experience, which contrasts sharply with our ordinary states of non-loving consciousness. It's obvious from the big deal that humans have made about love for millennia now—the epic songs, poems, novels, and movies—that the experience of love is unusual and special.

But even with all the attention that's been lavished on the experience, love is still extremely misunderstood. Love is defined in dictionaries as "strong affection for a person or thing" and "sexual passion or desire." Many believe love is an emotion provoked by encountering a loveable object; this belief is understandable because the only time we experience love is when we meet someone who matches the positives on our scale of value. A lot of us confuse sex and love, and end up in unhappy relationships because we thought sexual attraction meant we were in love. Others seem to think love is a behavior—love is what you do for others when you care about them.

Maybe we're so confused because, since love is extremely rare in most of our lives, we don't really know what we're talking about! Why is something that feels so wonderful so hard to find and hold on to?

We can "fall" into the experience of love when we come across someone who possesses an extraordinary number of positive traits on our scale of value. Yet, as we will see in the next chapter, it is that same scale that destroys our love. As long as we are living under the domination of subjective mind, love will be rare, brief, and restricted.

14

Love in the Age of Subjective Mind

The subjective mind perceives love as a mortal threat. Love, the experience of acceptance, the experience that everything has equal worth, is a refutation of the subjective mind's worldview.

Subjective mind survives by convincing us that value is relative and that most of reality is non-acceptable. Therefore some things are loveable but most things are not. One of the marvelous aspects of the love experience is that when you are in love, almost everything looks beautiful to you. It's easy to love a lover because the lover is not negatively value-judging the universe like the rest of us. It feels good to view life positively, to glow with happiness for a change. This contentment is a direct threat to subjective mind's survival, and it can't allow this experience to last.

Subjective mind works tirelessly to eradicate the experience of love in order to regain control. Subjective mind's principal love-destroying weapons are the subjective beliefs in free will and the relativity of value.

Imagine you have met someone who has set your bells to ringing: this person has an unusually large number of traits that are positive on your scale of value. You're in love!

Enjoy it while it lasts, because hard on the heels of any experience of love comes the first love-killing counter-attack, an understandable but nonetheless fatal reflex: the unwillingness to accept the possibility that our new love will end. We don't want love to go away! Unwittingly, we are being encouraged to kill our experience of acceptance with an obvious expression of non-acceptance. Subjective mind instills insecurity through the worry that our newfound happiness will vanish on us. We're like a starving person who is given an entire cake. It tastes delicious, but our initial delight is steadily eroded by a growing anxiety about finishing it—and winding up hungry again.

An even more potent weapon of the subjective mind is our scale of value; it may have spawned the experience of love, but it contains a fatal flaw. So what if our beloved has lovely eyes, a terrific personality, a great mind, and a sizable income? Is there not more to this person than this critical mass of positive traits, which brought about the love experience? Indeed there is, and our subjective mind—ever on the lookout for the negatives necessary to elevate and protect itself—will in time begin to uncover unacceptable traits in our beloved that become grounds for rejection. This means that whenever our love drifts outside our fixed parameters of acceptability, he or she is automatically judged to be non-acceptable; that is, non-lovable. The fixed and unyielding nature of our scale of value will eventually kill any love experience, because no person or object or circumstance can continually remain within the parameters of our rigid, unchanging beliefs about what is acceptable.

At this point our other major subjective belief—free will—kicks in. If our lover does something wrong, we think it's because they willfully chose to do it, therefore *they* are wrong. And how could we love someone who willfully chooses wrong and is, therefore, inherently wrong and lacking in worth? As we saw earlier, the belief in free will inevitably results in self-hatred; it will also inevitably result in hatred of our beloved.

Ordinarily it takes a long time for us to realize that our love has been destroyed (twenty years of marriage, say), due to our ability to delude ourselves by rationalizing, hoping, praying, ignoring, and dreaming that we're still experiencing love when we aren't (delusional: the state in which one kids oneself). This self-deception is commonly found in relationships where love has ceased to exist, but the ex-lovers sadly attempt to fool themselves and/or their partners into believing otherwise: "I love you"..."I love *you*." This clichéd exchange—rationalized to "spare the other's feelings"—is often sealed with a cold rubber-lipped kiss.

In families, expressions of love are hideously obligatory—you simply *must* act as though you are experiencing love whether it's true or not—so delusions about whether love exists among family members is commonplace.

And let's not forget (even though we'd very much like to), the impact of our self-hatred on our ability to love and be loved. Our negative self-appraisal demands an answer to the question, "How could this person possibly love someone like *me*?" As Groucho Marx once said, "I refuse to join any club that would have me as a member."

My husband Arthur wrote a country song (a response to the classic "Stand by Your Man"), which, in the first verse, describes the dilemma:

Well I don't care if you still say you love me
I simply don't believe it could be true
Two-thirds of who I am
Is someone *I* can't stand
So there must be something awful wrong with you!

In Edward Albee's play (and film) *Who's Afraid of Virginia Woolf*, Martha says of her husband, "George, ...whom I will not forgive for having come to rest; for having seen me and having said: 'yes, this will do'; who has made the hideous, the hurting, the insulting mistake of loving me and must be punished for it."[58]

One of the ways my self-loathing affects my ability to love is my irrational response to criticism: often when Arthur makes a comment about something I've done I hear it as a put-down when the truth is he's making a legitimate criticism, or even just a suggestion. Because of my belief, "only if I am perfect will other people love me," I'm terrified of Arthur ever seeing me as imperfect. This would mean he couldn't love me. So my subjective mind interprets even the mildest criticism as a threat to the future of our relationship.

I see this dynamic in other people's relationships, too. Recently we had a family over to watch a movie. At one point the young child knocked over an empty wine glass. When the man suggested to his wife that she move her full glass to a safer place, she reacted totally out of proportion. It was as if she heard him invalidating her worth as a human being because she did not think of putting her glass in a safer place herself. I saw myself all over that situation. I am always over-reacting to the slightest suggestion that I made a mistake (the very idea!). I am terrified of being exposed as the creep that I fear I am. I try so hard to be perfect because my subjective mind tells me that only when I'm perfect am I love-worthy.

At one point while writing this book Arthur and I had an experience of our mutual insanity and via that our equality—neither of us was the villain in our relationship. As a consequence we experienced a profound love for each other that continued for a couple of weeks. Then it disappeared. What happened? I know for one thing that I negatively value-judged Arthur when I saw him doing something I thought he shouldn't want to do anymore. In other words, I had expectations for how Arthur should behave following our love experience, and when I saw an old behavior pattern arise, I no longer accepted him. I, of course, blamed him: *his* behavior caused our experience of love to disappear. It was *because of* him. But the truth is his behavior was not what killed *my* experience of love; it was my non-acceptance that did it.

I often find myself blaming Arthur for being himself. I don't accept him the way he is. Over the years I have amassed a list of his traits that I consider to be negative, and I perceive those negatives as barriers to my loving him. I believe if he would simply change those aspects of himself, then I could really love him. Women are well known for this attitude. They talk about it among their friends: they marry a man and then improve him to their specifications.

I discovered that my love is contingent; my love depends upon the good behavior of the object of my love (myself included). If my beloved continues to behave in accordance with my scale of value, I will continue to express love. If, however, my beloved strays outside of my scale's fixed parameters, I will cease to express love. I am always watching to see if the object of my love behaves well enough to continue to "earn" my love. I am imposing a fixed scale of value on reality and when reality fits my scale, I love it, and when reality doesn't fit my scale, I don't love it. This goes for people as well as for things and events.

❖

In addition to our foundational subjective beliefs in free will and relative value, there are some other common beliefs that destroy any experience of love.

Our cultural myth about "true love" tells us that, when we find it, it won't go away: movies show a couple falling in love and riding off into the sunset; fairy tales end with "And they lived happily ever after." The obvious implication is that the couple will be in love forever; our culture teaches us that *true* love requires no effort. So when we fall in love, we believe we should never have any relationship problems, and, when we do, it is just because we haven't found Mr/Ms Right after all. So off we go—again—in search of the one who will be perfectly acceptable to us for all of time.

Other beliefs about love are concerned with attachment and action. Arthur wrote a song entitled "Because I Love You" that envisions an experience of love for all of humanity that doesn't require anything of another: "Because I love you doesn't mean I have to hold your hand/Or look into your eyes and try to make you understand." Recently he introduced the song at a small gathering by saying, "just because I'm feeling love doesn't mean I have to do anything about it," and it sounded as if all the women in the audience collectively groaned. I was shocked at how strongly these women were attached to the idea that love required relationship.

Most people think love is something special that is reserved for those we are connected to, either our family or our spouse/girlfriend/boyfriend/etc. It goes without saying we should love our family more than other people, right?

A friend of mine told his mother about a profound love he had experienced for a complete stranger. He tried to convince her that his spiritual experiences pointed towards a love that was universal instead of selective: that he could and should love her and everyone else on earth equally. She found this idea offensive and said something like, "Well, if you love any Joe Blow as much as you do me that love must not be worth much."

Our scale of value assigns higher value to that which is rare. Diamonds are more valuable than glass. Love is exceedingly rare for most of us and is, therefore, deemed highly valuable. Conversely, according to such logic, if love were commonplace, it wouldn't be worth much.

Another belief that confuses our understanding of love is the equation of love and sexual desire.

For many years I thought that if Arthur and I were having sex regularly then everything was fine with our relationship. Sex proved that love still existed between us. Sometimes after we'd had a fight and then a session of truth-telling to clear the air, we'd have great sex and even discover a new sexual position (which became our measure of whether we'd really worked through a problem). I mistakenly believed that the sex was what had re-established intimacy between us, when in fact it was just the side-benefit: the intimacy had been created through our being honest and open with each other as we resolved our argument.

As I've gotten older and my sex drive has declined, I've realized that sex can just create a mirage of intimacy and love. Sex can easily happen in the absence of intimacy. Intimacy requires that I stop hiding my true self from another. I've had a lot of trouble doing that in my life.

❖

Love dramatically disrupts our enslavement to subjective mind. Suddenly, we see what we've been missing. This is a direct threat to the negative-oriented subjective mind: maybe we'll catch on to the fact that love happens in the *absence* of subjective mind's value judgments.

Love is the experience of acceptance of what is. The fixed values of subjective mind sometimes allow us to experience acceptance, but as we've seen this experience will almost certainly be curtailed by the flaws inherent in the scale-of-value code-of-acceptability route to love. If we want love to last, we need to find another route to the experience of acceptance.

Part Three

Love is Sanity

15

The Pathless Path

Let's strip the ribbons and bows off our confused beliefs about love and consider the proposition that love is literally the state of sanity.

If love is sanity, then sanity can also be defined as: *the experience of unconditional acceptance of what is.*

Webster's defines "experience" as: *(philosophically) the totality of the cognition given by perception.*

It should be obvious that one can only experience something to the extent that one is cognizant, that is, aware, of it.

Some years ago I started keeping a journal. I lived in a rural area and walked in the woods regularly. When I first tried to portray what I had seen in words, I realized how little had registered in my awareness. I may have seen a patch of trillium, but how many flowers did I see—were there 15 or 50? What colors were they exactly? What variety of trillium did I see (there are 20 or so species in my area)? That fish I saw jump out of the stream—was it 8 inches long or 15? I obviously hadn't been fully present since I couldn't remember much detail.

In addition, I realized how much my flight/fight survival reflex affected my ability to see animals. One time I was picking blackberries and I saw a snake moving near me. I instinctively ran. I had no idea what kind of snake it was, even its color; all that registered in my awareness was "snake = run." When I was ten feet away I stopped and turned, and realized it was just a harmless black snake.

When I would sit in the woods, if I heard a sound I would instinctively turn towards it, and all I would ever see was the flash of a startled animal fleeing from me. I learned to stifle my response; when I heard a noise I would sit still, then very slowly turn my eyes in its direction. I was rewarded with many more sightings of animals—birds bathing in a stream, a muskrat swimming towards me, a rattlesnake curled up waiting in a blackberry bramble for a mouse, beavers paddling around their pond.

To experience something, not only do I have to perceive it, I have to accept it: to allow it to be, to exist, just the way it is. When I'm flighting and/or fighting, I'm rejecting what is; this rejection means I block the perception of what is; thus I cannot experience it.

Subjective value judgments are our flight/fight reflexes brought into the mental realm. To the extent that subjective value judgments—positive or negative—are imposed upon our objective perception of reality, our experience of reality is proportionately degraded.

When we tell someone to stop resisting a problem in their life, we say it's time for them to "face reality." Evolution has brought us to a level of awareness where we can contemplate a new response to stressful situations: we can face an issue instead of flighting or fighting. For example, say I made a mistake at work. This might cause me to get fired, so I have three options: (a) flight, which in this case might entail hiding the evidence of my mistake; (b) fight, which might entail getting angry and yelling at my secretary, making it look as if it was really someone else's fault; and (c) face, which would entail admitting that I had made the mistake and taking responsibility for doing whatever was needed to fix it, even if that meant being fired.

Thus our behavioral options are flight/fight/face. Facing reality means accepting it.

To accept reality does not mean lying down and letting reality run over us. If the snake we encounter in the woods is an aggressive rattler, flight or fight might well prove to be the best survival behavior, but facing objective reality would make these options far less likely. The objective fact is that most snakes are harmless and even the ones who pack venom are ordinarily more than willing to avoid confrontation. In fact, most people get bitten, scratched, and eaten because they are lost in a subjective mind-daze and not objectively aware of what's going on around them: they are not experiencing the here-and-now reality of their environment.

That rattlesnake I saw under the blackberry brambles is a good example. I was picking blackberries and came within a couple of feet of the snake before I saw her. By this point I had learned to look for snakes under blackberry branches and to be calm in the woods, so I saw her before I got too close for the snake's comfort. I also recognized that the snake had no interest in me: she didn't want to move and waste the time she had spent camouflaging her position. So I slowly backed away as we looked each other in the eye and she never even raised her tail in alarm.

In the same way, I can face a person's aggressive behavior instead of flighting from or fighting it, and actually experience a better outcome. I can also face my aggressive behavior instead of justifying it (my psychological flight/fight response).

For example, recently I caused a problem with a non-profit board. I had created an informational video for free as a contribution to the organization. During the development phase I had become irritated with some members of the board because they had given me very little feedback, but then the day came when the final video was shown at the annual meeting. That night I heard from a friend on the board, who said the response was mostly tepid, with some negative comments. I wrote her an angry email about how rude the board members were. I thought I was completely justified in my opinion and in my anger. It was self-evident to me that the members of the board were uncaring of my efforts. (The staff loved the video so I knew there weren't any major problems with my work.)

The next day I found out my friend had forwarded my email to the whole board because she agreed with some of my opinions. I was horrified because I had used some harsh language. An email from the president of the board showed I had really hurt her feelings. She also told me that I was mistaken in my assumptions about what happened at the meeting. I took immediate action, including making some phone calls and sending an email to the entire board apologizing for my unkind words.

I used to be a very stubborn person who would argue a point to death, mostly because I hated to ever admit I was wrong. If this had happened a few years ago I wouldn't have taken responsibility for precipitating a crisis when I received the email from the board president; I would have justified my actions and fought back. "I didn't do anything wrong," I would have claimed, "my friend was the one at fault for forwarding my email!"

But now I know I'm crazy. I recognized that I was confused in my thinking and had acted on faulty assumptions. I faced the reality of what was happening: I had jumped to conclusions without giving other people on the board time to comment to me directly, and I took my friend's comments at face value without considering whether she had some misperceptions of her own (which she admitted to later).

Realizing all of these things, and more, made it easy to write the email to the board apologizing for my angry words. Recognizing my insanity made it much easier to take responsibility for my actions.

When I accept that I am insane it removes the energy from the admission of fault. It doesn't mean I'm bad or evil. I was confused, that's all.

As counter-intuitive as it may seem, recognizing our insanity will boost our ability to be responsible for our lives.

❖

Experience requires awareness. To be aware of something requires us to be present in the here and now. But the filtration process that builds our mind-generated reality takes time, which means our awareness lags behind the present.

Actual reality (what is) logically occurs right now in the present moment. The word "present" has two relevant meanings: "here" *and* "now." The present is the absolute here and now. This is it. This is reality.

"Be Here Now" is a well-known spiritual exhortation. What this implies is that we are ordinarily *not* being, *not* here, and *not* now. Eastern metaphysical philosophy holds that thinking about reality removes us from the experience of reality—which only occurs in the present moment.

As we've seen, before we become consciously aware of reality it must pass through our mental filters. Trees, rivers, dogs, people, and chocolate bars must be delineated, located, defined, and assessed for value and meaning—all before they register in our awareness. All of this mental processing requires time.

Physical reflexes are lightning-fast because there is no mental processing involved. Involuntary reflexes do not require analytical or higher brain functions. When a doctor strikes your knee with a rubber mallet or you put your hand on a hot stove, the nerve impulses don't make it to the brain. They only go to the spinal cord where they trigger the appropriate response—the knee jerks or the hand moves. No thinking required. The involuntary reflex is a primordial response system that predates the higher brain functions. It continues to be a valuable pro-survival tool because in sudden crisis situations it allows the body to respond almost instantly.

Most of our activities require some mental processing and, as a result, include a time lag. As you read these words, there is a delay between the time your eyes receive the reflected light off the page (or screen) and the moment in which you comprehend what that reflected light means. Your mind has to perceive and interpret the light into the shape of letters, translate the letter combinations into words, the word combinations into a sentence, and the sentence into a comprehensible meaning. When we first learned to read, this time-delay was more obvious because each of these steps, due to our inexperience, required more processing time. While repeated practice has greatly accelerated the reading process, there is still a time lag between sight and comprehension.

This mental time lag is not insignificant, as Robert Pirsig asserts in *Zen and the Art of Motorcycle Maintenance*:

> You can't be aware that you've seen a tree until *after* you've seen the tree, and between the instant of vision and instant of awareness there must be a time lag. We sometimes think of that time lag as unimportant. But there's no justification for thinking that the time lag is unimportant—none whatsoever. The past exists only in our memories, the future only in our plans. The present is our only reality. The tree that you are aware of intellectually, because of that small time lag, is always in the past and therefore is always unreal. *Any* intellectually conceived object is *always* in the past and therefore *unreal*.[59]

By the time we become aware of any given event or thing we

have already processed it: objectively identified it, subjectively value-judged it, and forced it to conform to our mind-generated reality. By the time we have processed incoming sensory data the moment described by that sensory data has passed. As reality exists only in the present, what we are looking at is only a mental representation of a past reality.

Time appears to be relative because the amount of time-lag in our consciousness depends upon how much filtration (particularly subjective) is taking place in any moment.

Have you ever noticed that when you drive to a place you have never been before it seems to take forever, but once you become familiar with the route it seems to take much less time?

Why is this?

Imagine that you are driving to a new job for the first time and following somewhat complicated written directions. On this trip you are mentally *here and now*—you are (relatively) consciously present and accounted for. You are aware of the sights and sounds around you because your survival (your job) depends upon finding your way through unfamiliar territory in a timely manner. Your attention is required; you have to be more in the here and now present and thus you are far more conscious of the journey and all of the details in each passing moment along the way. You *experience* the trip.

Once you learn the way, however, the driving of this regular route is relegated to autopilot status, while more "important" data is given priority in your awareness. Instead of being present in the here and now you wander in the there and then (past or future) regions of your mind. This removes you from the present moment and makes the trip seem to go faster simply because you are much less consciously present to experience it.

Most of us can recall how a childhood summer seemed to last a geological age. Now, as an adult, a summer can flash by in an instant.

The world seems fresh and new to children because their evaluation filter is still under construction. They don't judge moments of now as lacking in value.

By the time we become adults we believe that virtually every new moment is comparable (and often identical) to past moments stored in our memory files. Our subjective mind tells us that *this* moment, because it is so similar to all *those* moments, does not really require our full attention. We become sophisticated—"I've seen it *all*, darling"—and we are bored.

Boredom is a completely delusional state: the truth is that we live in an ever-changing dynamic universe in which every moment is always new and deserving of our attention. Change is happening all the time but we don't see it because of the blinders of our subjective beliefs.

We reject reality when it doesn't conform to our ideas of what is valuable. I have beliefs about the worth of every moment of now: a vacation day is better than a workday, playing with my kids is preferable to taking out the garbage. So dreaming about how much fun I'm going to have this weekend while I'm cleaning the bathroom is a normal mental activity—who could possibly see scrubbing the toilet as a valuable moment of now? I imagine myself dancing in the club and the next thing I know the bathroom is clean, and I think it's a good thing that I got through it so quick. But that's a lie: I miss large chunks of my life because I don't experience every moment of now fully.

Time appears to speed up as we get older because when we live in a subjective mind-generated reality life passes us by unnoticed and unexperienced.

❖

Those of us who have experienced car wrecks—in particular those of us who have seen the collision coming—can attest to a very interesting phenomenon: *time appears to slow down.* This curious sensation is, of course, not unique to car crashes. However, it is most commonly noticed in life-threatening crises. More than one would-be suicide who has survived the jump from the Golden Gate Bridge has reported that the experience was "like falling forever."

Does time really slow down?

Let's create an analogy for our mind-generated reality: a one-seat theater in our minds in which we watch the film of our life. This film is scripted, edited, and directed by the beliefs and assumptions of our culture, time, family, and personal experience, and is projected on an internal screen of awareness.

Again, imagine you're driving your car to work. You're thinking about an argument you had with your boss yesterday. You enter an intersection, another car runs a stop sign, and a collision is unavoidable. What happens?

Just before the crisis begins, your awareness is focused on a vivid memory of the argument you had yesterday. You're looking at the scene in your mind's eye and feeling some anger and frustration ("I *should* have said..."). The driving of the car, which is happening in the present, has been demoted to a peripheral event that is being taken care of automatically. Your awareness is fixated on the past. You are watching a re-run of a memory movie on your internal screen of awareness.

The crisis situation suddenly and rudely pre-empts all irrelevant thoughts currently dominating your screen of awareness—in this case your memory movie—and in the process drags you out of the past and into the present. This is the equivalent of having your favorite soap opera interrupted by a news anchor screaming that nuclear war has begun.

When the crisis situation tears you away from your mind-movie and thrusts you towards the here and now you are given a rare opportunity to experience a shift in *time-awareness*. So rare is the true crisis moment that we are almost never given the chance to experience just how far behind the present we really are.

The closer we are to the present, the slower time appears. In the car accident, you are abruptly jerked from the past. Time appears to slow sickeningly because you suddenly begin to experience ever-changing moments of the present.

Each moment of now could be likened to a single frame of film passing through our mind's movie projector. When these frames are joined together and run sequentially in front of the projector's light, we are given a realistic representation of fluid, dynamic reality and the sensation of passing time.

As children, every frame of the reality movie fascinated us. As we grew older, we concluded that many of the new frames were so much like earlier frames that they no longer deserved our complete attention. As adults, we have seen the movie, My Story (starring me), so many times that it's very easy to become bored with it. The film begins to flash by with little or no attention given to entire scenes—much less single frames—and time seems to go faster. It appears as if the film is being fed through the projector at an ever-increasing rate of speed.

We begin to sleep through the movie of our life—one of the chief reasons there is so much regret as we near the conclusion of the film. A crisis situation is analogous to the film catching in the projector and permitting us to suddenly see individual frames. The effect is that of slow motion, of time slowing down.

If our life-film ever stopped completely, we would have attained the absolute present and, like attaining the speed of light, time would theoretically cease to exist. We all know what would happen then. The light of the projector would burn through the celluloid illusion and there would remain only white light.

❖

Recall the two laws of the universe: (1) Exist as Form and (2) Survive as Form. I'll now introduce a third: Transcend Survival as Form.

Evolution can be understood as the story of the transcendence of survival as form. For the first billion years (or so) of life on this planet there were only single-celled organisms. Each organism's primary survival identity was bounded by its cell wall.

The second chapter of life began when some single-celled organisms transcended their primary survival identity as individual cells and banded together to create multi-cellular forms. Their primary survival identity was no longer an individual cell, but that of a larger creature, at first simple algae or molds, then progressively more complex creatures like jellyfish and dinosaurs.

Human beings are a collection of approximately 10 trillion cells, all symbiotically working together to create a higher organization of organs and physiological systems.

But I don't think of myself as a group of living organisms working together; I think of myself as a singular "I." When some of my skin cells die and slough off, I don't think *I* have died. I have transcended survival *as* those cells. I don't think of myself as my body, I am something more. My body is the vehicle that allows *me* to operate in the world.

I think of myself as My Story. My subjective mind is my primary survival identity.

Throughout the eons of evolution on Earth, transcendence of survival as form happened very slowly, and, more importantly, was a completely unconscious process.

But now, for the first time (on this planet), a species has evolved which can *consciously* transcend its primary survival identity. Human beings have the unprecedented ability to be consciously aware that an option to their primary survival identity (subjective mind) exists.

For humans, "transcend survival as form" means to rise above limited subjective-mind awareness and enter a greatly expanded realm of awareness. We realize we are not our subjective mind; we *have* a subjective mind which allows us to operate in the world but it is not who we *are*. Who we are is something more.

Transcending survival as subjective mind means questioning my beliefs, which requires that I look at myself objectively. When I identify with My Story, I am surviving *as* it. I don't question it because I believe I *am* it.

When I realize that I am insane, I can recognize that my beliefs are just part of My Story; who I am is something else. Whatever that "else" may be, I'm not the collection of beliefs that make up My Story.

For example, one of the components of My Story is the belief that I must be perfect. I wanted everything about me to be perfect, including my physical body. As I result I have tried to eat right and exercise, which means overall I am extremely healthy. But whenever there was something wrong I would not see a doctor about it because I hated to have to admit that there was a flaw in my body. I put up with intermittent numbness in my right arm and leg for 20 years rather than admit there was something wrong with me. Finally I saw a chiropractor and he showed me how I was compressing some nerves through bad posture, and the numbness instantly disappeared.

Transcending identification with subjective mind means I will have the same feeling about having the thought, "I am so angry at that person I could kill him," as I do about the knobby growth on my thumb that just appeared. I may want to do something about my anger, just as I will (eventually) see my doctor about my thumb, but it isn't who I am, it doesn't mean anything about who I am. I don't think I'm a bad, evil person for having a bump on my thumb. I'm also not a bad, evil person for having an angry, hateful thought. I am not my thoughts just as I am not my farts!

Ken Wilber calls this process "Transcend and integrate." At every stage of human development we transcend identification with the earlier level, while integrating that level into the totality of our being. I have a body and I have a subjective mind; they are part of my totality, and I am something more.

One of the benefits of no longer identifying with my thoughts is that it's a lot easier to let them go. When I think they *are* me, I must take them seriously.

❖

Everyone has a subjective perspective of reality. Our individual subjective point-of-view is indispensable in a dualistic universe. As we have seen, what gets us into trouble is not the fact of our subjective point-of-view, or the content of our subjective mind, but rather the fatal assumption that our endless opinions, beliefs, and value judgments about the universe and ourselves are objective reality. This is the immediate source of our lunacy and the greatest threat to our continuance as a species.

Many of us were raised to believe that food equals love. Our mothers showed their love for us with special dinners and treats—cookies, cakes, and pies, oh my. We ended up overeating as adults because subconsciously we equated food with love and comfort. Many addictions are healed by abstaining from the addictive behavior, but food is a tough one because we can't stop eating! Food is required to exist in the physical realm.

So it is with the subjective mind. It has developed to the point that it dominates our awareness and often causes us to act self-destructively, yet we can't do without it—it's required for us to exist as discrete conscious creatures in a dualistic universe. Plus there are the many wondrous creations of our subjectivity: art and music for starters. The subjective mind is swollen beyond its proper size; it needs to be reduced to its proper dimensions; it needs to be healed and integrated.

A smaller subjective mind means an expanded conscious awareness: we are less involved in our own personal subjective world, and much more aware of the objective world around us. We recognize that what we see is not the truth of the universe but just our point-of-view.

For example, say I'm driving and someone cuts me off. When I'm less invested in my subjective point-of-view I don't just see my subjective reality—you made me miss the light, I'm justified in getting angry—I see the other person's too—maybe you are late for work and are worried about getting fired, maybe you just found out your mother is in the hospital and you're rushing to her bedside. I can see my subjective point-of-view objectively as just another point-of-view.

❖

There is an urgent need to take the problem of human insanity seriously. There are, at this writing, over seven billion people on this small planet, each dominated by a subjective mind that wants to be Number One. In fact, each subjective mind, the center of its own private world, says, "I *am* Number One." Every subjective mind is a self-centered, self-obsessed, self-justifying, self-rationalizing, self-promoting, self-protecting, self-perpetuating, self-fearing, self-hating *machine*.

This state of affairs, seven billion subjective-mind-dominated beings, each convinced that *they* are the fairest of them all, is not just another chapter in the history of human insanity. Technology—coupled with overpopulation—makes our time unique because it may well prove to be the *final* chapter of the Human Story. Seven billion subjective-mind slaves with seven billion conflicting mind-generated realities, armed to the teeth with guns, H-bombs, bulldozers, and chain saws, and the subjective value judgment systems to justify their implementation in the most selfish and irresponsible manner imaginable: from nuclear warfare to sweat shops to assembly-line genocide to the thoughtless destruction of the environment.

What is urgently required is the humility, respect, sanity, wisdom, and love that would flow from the objective realization that we are all delusional about reality.

Humanity is naturally moving in this direction. The question is whether enough of humanity will transcend identification with subjective mind in time.

Not so long ago there was a greater sense of community in the United States. We relied on one another. We had to. If my barn burned down, my neighbors would help me build a new one. And they'd expect me to return the favor should a similar misfortune befall them. There was more trust then. There had to be. We *needed* community in order to survive. A society is a system of cooperation, which, ideally, enhances survival for all of its participants.

Today if our barn burns down we call our insurance agent and an anonymous building crew comes out and puts up a new one. When the sun starts to set, our big screen TV provides us with all the companionship we could ask for. Better than human companionship, in fact, because we control the picture and sound, and our entertainment system never challenges our beliefs (if it does, we just change the channel). We have our own transport device that can take us anywhere we want to go. We have our own telephone, our own laundry, our own health insurance, and our own retirement plan. We can go on the Internet and have virtual sex and anonymous relationships. We don't need anyone else.

Modern technology allows us to escape the need to consider other people's viewpoints simply by giving us the unprecedented ability to insulate and isolate ourselves from others. We can live almost entirely for our own pleasure. Out in the world we may have to don the mask of cooperation and play the paycheck game, but once the car door slams, or the front door closes, we can be comfortably (safely) alone with ourselves.

When most people get in their cars, they feel so at home that they often display a complete lack of consideration for other drivers. People rarely act with such aggressive rudeness while walking down the sidewalk. All too common is the sight of a person alone in their vehicle, cell phone plastered to their head, angrily gesticulating at the unfortunate soul who has had the temerity to get in their way.

The technologically provided ability to be comfortably alone is a major contributing factor in the collapse of the institution of marriage. When things get tough, the modern person gets going...somewhere else. We are blissfully alone and autonomous, just the way our subjective mind likes it.

Today the United States is the ultimate example of instant gratification. No waiting! Next-day home delivery (in some locations: same day)! Everything all the time! 24/7! Never have so many had so much money and so many ways to spend it. Never has so much education and information been so widely available. Never has there been so much flexibility and freedom in dress, behavior, and manners. Anything goes. Morals are just what you like. Yet, despite all this brave new world of sensorial and behavioral carte blanche, large numbers of people are miserable and without purpose or hope (just look at the statistics for prescriptions of anxiety and depression medications, not to mention alcohol and drug abuse).

In earlier times, conformity was comparatively universal, because uniformity of behavior was required in order for a close-knit community to function. This meant suppression of any individual desires and impulses that did not adhere to the community standard (collective mind-generated reality). What's happening today is not the invention of new desires, just the ability to more openly express the old ones that have been there all along. Has anyone thought of anything really new in the realm of sexual expression that wasn't already explored in ancient Rome or chronicled in *The 120 Days of Sodom*, written in 1785 by the Marquis de Sade?

In the past, most people lived with the frustration of suppressed desires, believing they *could* have been happy if only they had been able to satisfy their cravings. But the majority lacked the courage to go against what seemed to be the only way to survive: conform to the tribal norm. Modern society has allowed us to increasingly indulge our individual desires, lusts, and impulses because we are accountable to almost no one.

We in the developed world are realizing, in unprecedented numbers, that satisfying our desires is not the key to happiness. We're learning that money *doesn't* buy happiness. This makes for an interesting—but dangerous—time.

To paraphrase Bob Dylan, "Your objective mind tells you what you *need*, but your subjective mind tells you what you *want*."[60] Objective awareness informs us when we have eaten sufficiently to maintain a healthy body. Subjective mind encourages us to cram our bellies until we groan, "I can't believe I ate the whole thing."

By indulging, by uninhibited gorging on the long-denied primal temptations, we are at last discovering, in critical numbers, the inherent lack of true satisfaction in the fruits of subjective mind. This period of indulgence is not a negative phase in the history of humanity, but instead a necessary step towards the evolved liberation from the madness of subjective mind.

❖

I have been interested in spirituality—and what I really mean by that is expanded consciousness—my entire adult life. But I have never followed a guru or joined any organization because I have been too distrustful of dogma. Who wants to spend years of your life submitting to someone's authority only to find out later that they were wrong?

I was frightened by mysticism because it sounded to me as though you're required to lose your identity and hang your mind up at the door. I couldn't understand why anyone would want to lose their ego and disappear. It appeared to me that an unquestioned truism of most spiritual traditions is that the mind is the chief obstacle to enlightenment. I loved intellectual pursuits, and I couldn't understand why anyone would want to abandon reason.

Another aspect of spirituality that I criticized was the common tendency of serious practitioners to withdraw from life. For many years I had a drawing on my wall of the Buddha seated in blissful contemplation in the midst of bustling Times Square. I wanted to find a way to be more conscious while participating in life fully.

As a result, I have carved out my own path, in conjunction with Arthur. I think of it as a "pathless path," because there's no dogma or beliefs to adhere to. The only goal is to be less insane.

In the next chapters I'll talk about some of the things I have learned on the pathless path.

16

Bend Like a Willow

The first lesson I learned is the wisdom of acceptance.

The subjective mind, because of its allegiance to fixed beliefs, is rigid and unbending: I would accept life when events went my way, but when they didn't, I'd reject whatever happened. Problems would cause me to "break"; I'd cry or feel despair or give up.

It occurred to me that maybe my problems weren't caused by things not going my way; maybe the problem was my rigidity, my unwillingness to accept reality as it is.

Reading Alan Watts' *The Wisdom of Insecurity* helped me understand this principle. This passage about acceptance jumped out at me: "[Taoism] showed how the supple willow survives the tough pine in a snowstorm, for whereas the unyielding branches of the pine accumulate snow until they crack, the springy boughs of the willow bend under its weight, drop the snow, and jump back again."[61]

I made "bend like a willow" my mantra, which means, "bow to the reality of whatever is before me."

Bend like a willow is my visual representation of acceptance: as a willow bends in the wind so that even the strongest gust can't break it, so I can bend with the events that flow my way and allow them to move through and past me without breaking me. In flexibility there is strength.

Some years ago I was using a box-cutter and severely cut my right hand along the fleshy edge below the little finger. The cut was two inches long and quite deep. My doctor told me I had missed cutting the tendon for the little finger by millimeters (she showed me the exposed tendon while she was assessing the wound).

The most interesting thing about the experience had to do with acceptance. As I stood over the bathroom sink, where I had immediately run after slicing myself open, I stamped my foot in anger. Arthur said, "No getting angry at yourself," and as he drove me to the doctor I settled into the reality of the situation. Arthur and I talked about accepting the objective reality of my injury while we waited for the doctor in the surgery room, and by the time she arrived we were both in a state of acceptance. Later we joked that people outside the room would think the three of us were having a party. I didn't take the tranquilizer the doctor offered and watched, fascinated, as she sewed me up. We told stories and laughed (this was our family doctor, we had known her for years). She stitched the underlying muscle first, and I could feel a deep sensation of renewed wholeness as she completed those stitches. She told me that I wasn't supposed to be able to feel sensations in that layer, and I wondered if my calmness—the result of my attitude of acceptance—allowed me to experience it.

❖

True acceptance goes much farther than the resigned "things are the way they are and there's nothing I can do about it" that many of us associate with the idea of acceptance: a passive attitude towards the pain and suffering of life. True acceptance includes a sense of fulfillment and satisfaction in the way things are; no longer having any expectation or desire that this moment be any other way than exactly the way it is. True acceptance welcomes the bad with the good as equally essential aspects of life in a dualistic universe. As a friend once wrote in an email, life is "simultaneously tragic and beautiful." Celebrate that.

Acceptance is consenting to what I have been given in life. Not resentful of the gifts I didn't receive, or envious of the talents others have that I don't, or bitter about my weaknesses and flaws. Acceptance allows me to see the world as an enormous puzzle, with each organism a uniquely shaped piece, each having its perfect place in the interconnected picture. Acceptance means I stop trying to be a different piece of the puzzle. True acceptance means I feel gratitude for the way it is.

A friend once told me a parable of enlightenment: God was touring the world visiting seekers after truth. God came to a man who had been meditating 18 hours a day for 20 years. God said, "Yes,

yes, you're doing well but you still haven't gotten it." God went on and visited a woman who had devoted her life to the poor and worked selflessly for 30 years. God told her, "You have done great works but you still don't understand." Then God saw a man who had been striving after enlightenment for 40 years, who had deprived himself of all things worldly in order to attain spiritual rewards. God said, "You've put your attention on the wrong things." Finally God came upon a woman dancing in a meadow, ecstatic at the sheer beauty of existence, not just accepting the way it is but *satisfied* with the way it is, not wanting it to be any other way. God cried, "She gets it!" And she was instantly enlightened.

Alan Watts also uses the analogy of dance to explain acceptance:

> [Life] is a dance, and when you are dancing you are not intent on getting somewhere. You go round and round, but not under the illusion that you are pursuing something, or fleeing from the jaws of hell...The meaning and the purpose of dancing is the dance. Like music, also, it is fulfilled in each moment of its course. You do not play the sonata *in order* to reach the final chord, and if the meanings of things were simply in ends, composers would write nothing but finales...When each moment becomes an expectation life is deprived of fulfillment, and death is dreaded for it seems that here expectation must come to an end.[61]

Acceptance means no longer imposing my subjective expectations on reality. When I realize that I'm insane, I recognize that my subjective mind-generated reality is delusional. Part of the delusion is the belief that life has to follow my subjective mind's script. I can stop the rigid two-step I've been doing and dance spontaneously with life as it is.

❖

The idea of complete acceptance of reality first hit me as a dangerous prescription for being a doormat. As a "liberated" modern woman, I'm alert to anything that smacks of justifying the passivity that is part of traditional female behavior. Am I to accept a person who attacks me? Does acceptance mean that I let anyone do anything they want to me? Do I just let bad things happen without taking any action?

These common prejudices about acceptance are wrong. In fact, acceptance of reality greatly enhances my ability to act and survive in the world.

As we've seen, in our ordinary state of consciousness our perception of reality is greatly distorted by our subjective value judgments and beliefs, so our experience of what is happening around us is limited. How effective can we be in our response to events if we do not accurately perceive them? When we accept reality it means that we perceive reality more accurately, thus our ability to act is improved.

This is the philosophy behind martial arts, and particularly Aikido, a non-aggressive system of self-defense (not that I know this by any involvement in martial arts myself, this opinion is strictly from reading). Aikido training involves learning to perceive, accept, and exploit reality to your survival advantage. By objectively seeing the dynamics of an attack you have the ability to use the energy of your attacker to move him or her beyond you while expending as little of your own energy as possible. The more accurately you perceive and accept the exact configuration of an attack, the easier it is for you to deal with it.

When we are subjective-mind-dominated we are compelled to act in accordance with our subjective mind-generated reality, and our delusions about reality render our actions confused and ineffectual. It is as if we suffer from cataracts *and* wear blinders: what we do see of reality is blurred by our preconceptions, and there are huge sections of reality that we don't see at all. In the experience of acceptance our cataracts are removed and the blinders are opened wide; we see reality far more clearly and are therefore better equipped to deal with it.

Many years ago when I lived in San Francisco I worked at night and rode the bus home. I never had any troubles, even though sometimes I had to wait for a bus on downtown streets at midnight and was almost always the only female at the bus stop. I think the reason for my lack of problems was that I believed my safety depended on my alertness to the situation around me at all times. Whenever I arrived at a bus stop I would look around me and let the other people know (non-verbally) "I am here waiting for my bus and you're here waiting and you should leave me alone."

Interestingly, the only time a scary situation arose was during the day. I was at a crowded stop in Chinatown, and a man came and stood uncomfortably close to me and stared at me. I moved and he moved with me. We threaded through the clot of people and by the time the bus arrived I knew I had a problem. I sat down next to someone so the man couldn't sit by me, but he stood in the aisle right next to me and continued staring. As soon as the seat in front of me emptied out he sat there and turned and stared.

It became clear that I had to take action or he would follow me home, and who knows what would happen once I was away from other people. So I said in the loudest voice I could summon, "I am tired of you following me and staring at me. Leave me alone." He weakly protested, "I'm not staring at you," but at the next stop he jumped up and got off.

I was embarrassed at speaking like this in front of all the people on the bus, but I wondered later how many women have been raped because they were unwilling to admit what was happening and/or were unwilling to accept a little embarrassment to call attention to their situation.

Acceptance of reality is always empowering.

❖

In the subjective-belief trance that is our ordinary state of consciousness we think the only way to accept reality is when it fits our pictures of what's acceptable. We think being willing to accept "negative" situations is a recipe for disaster. Surely there can be nothing positive in a negative!

I love the film "Pleasantville" because it illustrates that without conflict there is no life.[62] In the film, Pleasantville is the name of a 1950's television sitcom about a town where nothing bad ever happens and everything is always the same; there's no anger or conflict or loss; everything is always "pleasant." But it's also a place where there is no joy or love or art or growth. Everything is black-and-white; there is no color.

Two teen-agers from the 1990s are magically transported into the show. They question the reality that everyone in Pleasantville takes for granted, and change starts to happen. The first thing the Pleasantville kids discover is sex, and the new feelings of sensuality allow them to experience color. They quickly turn to books: they want to explore, learn, and grow. As they expand their minds, color, joy, love, and art spread through the population. But that also brings the new experiences of anger, pain, loss, and violence. The film ends with a character saying: "It's not supposed to be any way." That is, there's no perfect place without problems. It's supposed to be just as it is: our dualistic universe is a mix of joy and loss.

For fifteen years I lived in a mountain valley. People owned property along the road but the mountains above were part of a national forest. I carved my own trails up the mountainsides and spent many happy hours traversing my private mountains (I never saw another soul in all my treks). For years I hiked to the tops of the mountains, but then one winter I felt like something new. Between Big Dog and Rattlesnake Mountains (I didn't make these up—they are the official names!) was an incredible saddle with a ridgeline so narrow that when I walked along it in winter I could see far-off mountains to the left and right. One day it occurred to me to walk down the "trough" between the two mountains.

Just below the saddle I found a little rivulet where it sprang up from its springhead. I followed it as it spread out over autumn leaves and began falling over rocks. As I descended, the brook got wider, spilling over larger boulders and forming pools. Finally I got to the bottom of the mountain and the stream entered a rhododendron forest and I turned back.

As I climbed back up to the saddle I thought: In life we are always seeking the highs—the great moments, the pleasures, the peak experiences. We shun the troughs—the sad times, grief, despair, loss. But as in Pleasantville the highs and the lows are contingent; you can't have one without the other. I had missed the beauty of this mountain trough because I was sure the mountain peaks were of most value as a destination.

When I spoke about this to Arthur, he said, "Does this keep us stuck in a 'comfortable' situation because at least it's 'pleasant'? Are we afraid to take risks because it might lead to a trough?"

❖

Another mantra: Expect Craziness.

Now that I understand that everyone is insane, it's no longer a surprise when people act crazy. This makes it much easier to accept the craziness in the world. If a friend acts weird, I don't take it personally—she's insane. I don't know what's really going on in her mind. When my neighbor does something ridiculous, I don't get angry—he's nuts. Expect people to do crazy things because they *are* crazy.

When I expected people to act sanely I was constantly disappointed or irritated. I rejected huge swaths of life.

This mantra applies to the larger culture and world, not just to individuals. Marijuana is illegal while alcohol is legal? Craziness. North Korea wants to use a nuclear weapon to threaten the United States? Craziness. The United States borrows from China to finance a military to contain China? Craziness. Climate change is happening and might result in the end of human civilization, if not the human race, but we can't muster the political will to do anything about it? Craziness. Billions of people live in utter poverty while a tiny handful live in decadent luxury? Craziness.

These are examples of things that would, in the past, cause me to start raving with anger and outrage. I would self-righteously accuse people involved of all sorts of evil intent.

Today I recognize them as components of an unavoidable phase of human evolution; inevitable expressions of the confusion of subjective beliefs with objective facts. This is what happens when crazy people run world affairs. I would submit that through acceptance and understanding of insanity there is a much higher chance of finding solutions to these issues than through anger and blame.

❖

How do I know if I'm bending like a willow? I've found a simple way to tell if I'm accepting reality in any given moment: if I feel agitated in any way I'm not accepting what's going on. If I'm angry, irritated, bored, jealous, disappointed, or anxious I'm not bending to what is. I see my emotional state as a precise minute-to-minute gauge of my state of acceptance. I don't need anyone or anything outside myself to clue me in to where I'm at—that's what my emotions are for!

A good part of my anxiety comes from envisioning future possibilities that don't exist in the present moment and may never manifest. I have learned that by keeping my attention on the present, accepting what is, doing my best with what I know in this moment, and not imposing mental images of what might be, I am much more successful in solving problems. Part of the reason I am more successful is that I haven't wasted a lot of energy worrying about a future that never happens.

17

Question My Story

For most of my life I hated the idea of humility. For me humility was synonymous with humiliation—and for good reason. Here are some synonyms of "humility" from an online dictionary: docility, fawning, inferiority complex, lowliness, self-abasement, servility, subservience, and timidity. Our language seems to show that we as a culture have a very low opinion of humility.

For me, humility meant admitting, "I don't know" or "I'm wrong"; I hated this because, according to My Story, I'm too smart and perfect to be humble!

The more I have learned about insanity and the inherent limits it imposes on my knowledge of reality, the more I have understood the folly of resisting humility.

Humility just means the willingness to acknowledge the extent of my ignorance and lack of objectivity: to face the truth of just how much there is that I don't know and how often I pretend to know when I don't. Humility is achieved through my willingness to honestly face, and thus experience, my limitations.

When we're insane we are unaware of our limitations: we are ignoramuses. I once saw this definition of "ignoramus": *a vain pretending to knowledge*. We are not ignoramuses when we admit to our ignorance, that is, when we're humble and acknowledge the objective fact of our limitations. We are ignoramuses when we believe and/or act as though we know when we don't know.

In a *Three Stooges* episode Larry sits down at a formal dinner table, notices the small crystal fingerbowl at his place setting, exclaims with delight, and proceeds to use it for an eye cup, merrily rinsing both eyes in front of his astonished fellow diners. A person who was aware of his ignorance, who was uncertain of the purpose of the fingerbowl, would have asked for help or waited and watched for a clue. Ignoramuses like Larry plow boldly ahead in the self-delusion that they know what they're doing.[63]

The oracle at Delphi named Socrates the wisest man in Athens. Socrates rhetorically asked, "How can I be the wisest man in Athens if I know nothing?" The answer, of course, was that Socrates was the only man in Athens who *knew* he knew nothing (in the absolute sense)—and thereby knew more than the rest of the population! Socrates had humility.[64]

The first step towards sanity is to face the painful truth, "I *don't* know." Humility is a denial of, and a direct threat to, the arrogant position which subjective mind maintains: "I know who I am; I know what I'm doing."

Why do we fear the statement "I don't know"? Because ignorance is the source of all fear. This is why children have such a hunger to learn: knowledge is equated with survival and the lessening of fear. Unfortunately, what we learn is a narrow, distorted, and fixed view of the universe that our culture teaches is essentially "all we need to know" in order to get through life.

G. Spencer Brown wrote, in an appendix to his classic work of mathematics and philosophy, *Laws of Form*: "In our system of education, we are taught to be proud of what we know and ashamed of what we don't know. This is doubly corrupt."[65]

Our culture values pride; we're taught to have self-esteem in school; meekness is scorned while self-confidence is worshiped.

There's a classic Zen story about a man who goes to the master and asks him to teach him Zen. The master says, "Let's have tea first," and begins to slowly pour tea into the man's cup. The cup gets fuller and fuller and the man becomes increasingly agitated as he watches the tea reach the brim and then begin to overflow onto the table...and then onto the floor! Finally, when he can no longer stand it, the man cries, "Stop! The cup is full!" "So is your mind," the master replied. "Go and empty it, and then I can teach you Zen."[66]

There's no room for meaningful growth in a mind that knows it all (including the standard know-it-all mind clever enough to say, "Of course I don't know it all! I never claimed to!"). Only the mind that can *experience* "I don't know" is free to learn. A mind that says "I know" when it doesn't know has a fortified position to defend and an entrenched bias which reality must conform to. There's no space for learning. The mind is full.

Subjective mind's survival depends upon its ability to convince us that we "know all we need to know," and "of course we don't know it all, but we damned sure know what we know!" Remember, if a belief can be identified as incorrect, it loses its structural integrity, it changes, and it "dies" as its former self. Subjective mind, therefore, perceives "I don't know" as a deadly threat, and as long as we identify with our subjective mind we will feel the same way.

Accepting my insanity is guaranteed to evoke humility—you can't be any humbler than nuts! As long as I cling to my threadbare pride all I'm left with is the hope that someday My Story will have a happy ending. Only when I objectively acknowledge my insanity can I face the tyrant of subjective mind and its defensive shield of self-hatred. Only then can I effortlessly answer the darkest self-accusation with "Hey, I'm crazy! What do you expect, sane behavior?"

❖

As I have realized how much I have confused my subjective opinions with objective facts, I have naturally begun to question My Story. My Story is largely made up of subjective opinions; what if I stop taking them at face value? What if I stop assuming that the contents of my mind are true?

The description I've given of My Story thus far has shown that I'm obviously deluded about a lot of things. The realization of my insanity has given me the incentive to challenge some of my basic assumptions about reality.

Some years back I befriended a wonderful mountain woman named Hazel. I loved spending time with her. She turned 90 when I was 45, and I was stunned when I realized that she had lived two of my lives.

When I contemplated all of the life I had lived up to that point—from the infancy that I couldn't even remember, through childhood, teen-age angst, college years, the wild adventures of my twenties, to the more sober work-life of my thirties and forties—I was overwhelmed at the opportunity of living that much time again. (I come from a long-lived family so it is very possible that I will live to be 90.)

This was a very profound event for me, because it caused me to ask myself what I wanted the second half of my life to be like. At that time Arthur and I were developing the theory of universal insanity, which gave me the insight that in order to change my life I needed to seriously question my mind-generated reality.

Did I want to continue listening to My Story? Did I want to keep playing it weak? Did I want to always be a pathetic victim of circumstances? Did I want to go on playing the dominated woman, ruled by a man? Did I want to keep playing it like a loser? Did I want to be a ghost my whole life?

At about this time Arthur and I began broadcasting the weekly television show I mentioned earlier. The first year looked familiar: Arthur was the camera operator and he set the agenda for filming and editing: what we covered, how long we stayed at an event, etc. I was just an all-purpose assistant, my long-term role.

But I was dissatisfied with the results we produced, and during the second season I began to assert myself. I filmed and edited events and interviews by myself so they would be done the way I wanted them done. By the time we stopped producing the show five years later, I was doing it almost completely by myself. The show was very popular in town and for most people I was the sole face of the show.

During this time I started writing a weekly opinion column in the local newspaper (small towns are great for giving you the chance to contribute). This was a relatively conservative town, and my column was distinctly liberal. Over three years I got progressively more willing to state my opinions in print. It was hard at first because some of the letters written in opposition to my columns were personally abusive. But I also heard comments like, "I don't agree with your liberal opinions but I always read your column because it makes me think about things from a new point-of-view."

My new assertiveness caused conflict with Arthur. All of a sudden I wasn't playing the same old part in our relationship game. I felt like I had to act tough to keep from sliding back into my habitual behaviors, and Arthur interpreted that to mean I didn't love him anymore and wanted to leave him.

He would quote the memorable line from *The Serial*, the 1970's satire of Marin County, "She was still confusing being a liberated woman with being a nickel-plated bitch!"[67]

I also over-reacted at times, thinking I had to fight to get free. I didn't allow for the possibility that Arthur wanted me to be free, really, and it was just *his* subjective mind that wanted me to stay in my passive role. Sometimes I thought I was going to hurt his feelings by wanting to go out alone and a drama would ensue, and later I would realize that the drama was created (at least in part) by my fears of expressing my strength.

By the time we moved away from this small town I felt like a butterfly that had emerged from its chrysalis. I had learned that My Story was *wrong*: I'm not a loser. I'm not weak. I had created a successful, popular television show and a well-read newspaper column, and I was something of a celebrity in the small town. Arthur said, "We can't go anywhere without someone wanting to have a conversation with you."

This isn't to say I don't still hear that old Story in my head—I do. But I've discovered the power in questioning it. Now when my inner narrator tells a "loser" or "weakling" story I mostly remember to say, "Thanks for sharing, subjective mind, but no thanks."

The only way to question My Story is to step outside the subjective mind and look at it objectively. Every waking moment, and dreaming moment for that matter, is an opportunity to discover a more objective vantage point: a place where I am detached from automatic acceptance of whatever explanation of reality my subjective mind is currently serving up.

❖

Subjective mind is a powerful storyteller. Its power is such that it can easily convince its host that pain is good, that wrong is right, that weakness is strength, that hate is love. Seeing hate as hate is a matter of objective observation, of telling the truth about it. The way to tell the truth about whether we're feeling love or hate is to question the story. Questioning the story begins with saying, "I don't know if this is true or not"; entertaining the possibility that we might be mistaken.

How can I question the beliefs of subjective mind when they are part of the filter through which I see reality? How do I know whether a belief is true or false?

A belief is false to the exact extent to which it fails to admit to its limitations.

I am insane to the exact degree to which I am unaware of the limitations of my mind-generated reality. In order to be (relatively) sane, I have to be aware of my limitations. To be aware of my limitations is to be humble. Since the only thing we know absolutely is "something's happening," humility is always appropriate. All of our knowledge is limited! To the extent that I'm consciously aware of my limitations—of how little I know absolutely—I'm in good shape; I have my feet on the solid ground of objective reality. The times I find myself absolutely certain of my position, the times I absolutely know that I'm right without any doubt, these are the times I'm in trouble.

Arthur C. Clarke provides a stunning case in point: "Who can forget Jacob Bronowski, in his superb TV series *The Ascent of Man*, standing among the ashes of his relatives at the Auschwitz crematorium and reminding us: 'This is how men behave when they believe they have absolute knowledge.'"[68]

Or to quote Confucius: "When you know a thing, recognize that you know it. And when you do not know a thing, recognize that you do not know it. That is wisdom."[69] And, we can add, that is humility and sanity.

Humility is simply realizing "Hey, I'm limited!" This observation would be absurdly obvious and effortless were it not for the fact that I'm crazy. And by "realizing" I mean *experiencing* I'm limited. Remember that talking about love and experiencing love are two very different states. What I'm after here is experience. It's not enough for me to say, "I'm limited," I have to *experience the reality of it.* Only when I experience my limitations am I free of the arrogance of subjective-mind domination.

I have found a good place to start is just to question everything the mind spits out. "Do I *really* know that?" "Is that really true or is it just my opinion?" I try to remember to say, "In my humble opinion..." and actually *mean* it!

Humility has had a powerful impact on my life. In the past, because I felt like I needed to be perfect to be accepted, I couldn't laugh at myself. I took myself very seriously, and, when I made a mistake, was quick to hide it or rationalize it. Now I am almost always able to laugh at myself and admit my flaws and faults to others, which makes me much less stiff and formal.

I also used to think I knew how others should live their lives, and was always ready with unsolicited advice and/or unspoken criticism. I believed I knew what was best for their lives, and if they didn't follow my advice I would get angry. Now I recognize that I have only a narrow idea of what it is like to be them. My understanding of their inner motivations and the pressures they endure (both internal and external) is necessarily limited and not the absolute truth. As a consequence, I have stopped thinking and acting like I know better, and the space I am now giving to the people in my life has resulted in closer relationships with them.

I don't say things like "I understand what you're feeling" any more, because I can't ever fully understand another (I don't fully understand myself!). I say, "I think I understand," and that little word "think" makes all the difference.

❖

A note to myself: *Include other people's reality.*

When I first had this thought, "include other people's realities," it seemed like it had to be mistaken; it sounded like it meant I should believe their mind-generated reality was the truth.

Every October our house in the mountain valley would be invaded by Asian lady beetles. These insects, we were told, had been released by the U.S. Department of Agriculture as a "natural" control for aphids on pecan trees. In their native habitat these beetles migrated to mountain caves in the fall where they would spend the winter huddled in tight balls for warmth; in this country they substituted houses for the caves. Every fall literally thousands of these beetles would crawl through the cracks in the old farmhouse walls and take up residence in the attic, coming out every sunny afternoon to swarm in the windows. I found it annoying, but for Arthur these beetles were an annual disaster.

Every fall he would get angry about the beetles, and every fall I would get angry with him, because I thought he was exaggerating his reaction. Then one year I stopped projecting my reality ("it's annoying") and really listened to what he was saying ("it's a nightmare"). I realized that the arrival of the beetles induced something like a panic attack. Arthur wasn't just being dramatic when he used the word "nightmare," he was really suffering. I moved from condescension and irritation to compassion and service—I was ready to help him take care of the problem.

Accepting Arthur's reality that "the beetles are a nightmare" didn't mean I believed that his interpretation represented *actual* or even *objective* reality. I simply recognized that "the beetles are a nightmare" was Arthur's subjective perception of reality. When I better understood his mind-generated reality I could relate to him much more compassionately and effectively.

I've also realized that disagreements often can be boiled down to "my perception of reality is right and yours is wrong." When arguing, I reject another's reality and focus on asserting and justifying my reality. If I can accept that we are both operating from mind-generated realities, I can conceive the possibility that the truth exists somewhere between our two versions, or even that it's something completely different.

Werner Erhard, the founder of est, wrote many aphorisms. One that has stuck with me in the 30 years since I did the est training is, "The essence of communication is intention, and you can tell your intention by the results produced."[70] We can't know all that is in our mind, but we can know what manifests in objective reality. Did a conversation with Arthur about the future of our business turn into an argument? That means that there was something in my mind that blocked acceptance of his reality. What was it?

Once again, I'm not saying that I need to be a doormat that just lets anyone have their way to avoid conflict. I'm saying that if we start shouting at each other in anger over our disagreement, clearly there is something else going on. Why am I angry?

As I said in the last chapter, emotions and actions are the clue to my inner state of consciousness. Am I accepting what is, or do I have some internal agenda that I am imposing on this moment of now?

18

Clean Sex

Living a conscious life (I use that term for lack of a clearer alternative; I am trying daily to live a more mindful, accepting, humble life) means that over time more and more areas of your life are brought into the circle of your discipline (that is, there is no differentiation between your "spiritual" path and what you do in your daily life). Eventually this includes your sexuality.

It seems to me that many people are convinced that spirituality and sexuality are opposites and that the only way to deal with sex is to abstain. This might explain why I had so much trouble finding any reference to sex in the spiritual books I read. I have never accepted this separation as true. In fact, this attitude is based on a subjective belief that there is a separation between the physical and the spiritual; that they are two completely separate spheres of existence. I don't think there is any difference between the two. I like Alan Watts' attitude: "Matter is spirit named."

I once read a story about a man who was trying very hard to be pure in his spirituality and as a consequence lived an extremely ascetic life. He went to a meditation retreat with his wife and the teacher took one look at him and said, "You will spend this week in your room with your wife having sex." The man objected, "that's not why I came here," but the teacher insisted. At the end of the week the man was glowing; he had discovered that spirituality does not mean the rejection of the physical.

Most modern cultures' consensual reality about sex is restrictive and negative. In the United States where I live, the culture's beliefs include: monogamy is the only acceptable sexual relationship, sex should be done in private, sex is dirty (which is why it needs to be hidden), men like sex more than woman, women who like sex are sluts or nymphomaniacs, it's wrong to feel aroused, we should feel shame about our desires, etc.

Modern American culture is sex-obsessed, yet prudish—a prurient Puritanism. In other words, very confused. Fifty years after the so-called sexual revolution our culture is still extremely conflicted about sex (to put it mildly).

Sex is obviously a natural part of life! Reproduction is the basic mechanism of life. Our sexuality is as basic a part of our physicality as our appetite for food. Yet most of us hide our sex lives; it's the part of life we can't discuss openly. We can share all sorts of things with our friends—eating, dancing, shopping, watching films, going to concerts, skydiving, week-long treks—but there's one thing that's off that list: sex. And if we do share sex with our friends, we often end up ruining at least one relationship.

Because of our cultural beliefs about sex we believe that if we're in a committed relationship and feel desire for another person that means something's wrong with our relationship: it must mean we want out of the relationship or the other person is not satisfying us. We think we have just two choices: hide our desire and live with our frustration or cheat by having an affair.

Because of our cultural beliefs about sex we believe that we should feel shame about our sexual desires. Someone who has spent many years as a mentor in Alcoholics Anonymous said that when it gets time for people to do the fourth step, which entails making a "searching and fearless moral inventory," the hardest part for the hundreds of people he had worked with was being honest about their sexual conduct. These were people who had done all kinds of unethical behavior in the course of their drinking, and robbing or cheating was effortless to confess compared to details of their sex lives.

Because of our cultural beliefs about sex we believe that men like sex more than women. I was indoctrinated with this in the 1960s, but I thought this was one belief the sexual revolution had put an end to. But from recent accounts by young women that is not the case. An enterprising young woman was putting herself through Duke University by starring in online porn videos until someone recognized her on campus. She wrote an essay that confirmed this cultural belief still exists in full force, just as it did in my youth:

> My entire life, I have, along with millions of other girls, been told that sex is a degrading and shameful act. When I was 5 years old and beginning to discover the wonders of my body, my mother, completely horrified, told me that if I masturbated, my vagina would fall off. The most striking view I was indoctrinated with was that sex is something women "have," but that they shouldn't "give it away" too soon—as though there's only so much sex in any one woman, and sex is something she does for a man that necessarily requires losing something of herself, and so she should be really careful who she "gives" it to. The prevailing societal brainwashing dictates that sexuality and sex "reduce" women, whereas men are merely innocent actors on the receiving end. [71]

This brings up another relic of our cultural beliefs about sex: most people don't even know what to call a woman's genitalia. The mother above called it a vagina. I myself didn't know until recently that the correct name is "vulva."

These are all cultural subjective beliefs about sex, which we have incorporated into our personal subjective realities without question. They are not objectively true.

The explosion of Internet pornography and the obvious contribution of sexual problems to our high divorce rate makes it clear to me that it's time to take a good look at our cultural beliefs about sex. Why is sex dirty? What's wrong with a woman enjoying sex? What is so special about monogamy? Why do we have to hide our sexual feelings?

Every time a politician gets caught in a sex scandal the absurdity of our culture's attitudes is on display. When Anthony Weiner was caught tweeting a photo of himself in his underwear, he was forced to resign from Congress. Why? Eliot Spitzer had to resign as governor of New York because he visited prostitutes. Why? Bill Clinton was almost impeached for a blowjob. Why?

Maybe if we got over our puritanical attitudes toward sex and allowed more freedom for people to express themselves sexually (other than privately with one partner at a time) we'd have fewer of these scandals, and fewer marriages would end because of an affair.

Why can't men (and women!) legally visit prostitutes? Why can't we act on the sexual connection we feel with certain people in our lives, even if it's only a one-time experience, and not have it *mean* anything? Why isn't polygamy legal? What's wrong with having ongoing sexual relationships with more than one person?

❖

As I mentioned in the My Story chapter, for many years I struggled with sex. I wanted to know: how does sex change as you grow in consciousness? What is appropriate sexuality and what is addictive or compulsive sexuality? How do I separate out loving from lusting? How can I love others without sexuality intruding in an unconscious way? How can I be a sexual being without it controlling me?

I can't say I have answers to all of these questions, but I'll share what I have discovered.

I was a teen-ager during the 1970's and was greatly influenced by the "free love" philosophy of the time. I don't know why but it made sense to me that sex could be separated from committed relationship. Perhaps I saw it as an extension of women's liberation: women had been enslaved for centuries in monogamous relationships where they had to be sexually true to one man. The only way to be truly liberated would be to be free sexually also.

Not only did I think free love meant I could have sex with whomever I wanted, I also thought it meant sex could be liberated from being "dirty." My image of free love was always "clean," that is, it was about loving the one you're with—whoever that happened to be. I thought sex should be, and was, beautiful.

When I was in my twenties I acted on my belief in free sex. I traveled to the Soviet Union in 1979, during the height of the Cold War, when I was 21 (I could speak Russian), and had sex with a number of Russian men during my travels. I was engaged in my own personal form of détente—and I have a feeling that practiced on a large enough scale, this form of détente could bring about the peace that has eluded ordinary diplomacy.

Arthur and I have had sex with a number of different people, sometimes with just one person and sometimes with more than one.

We were never into the "swinger" scene, we didn't have anonymous sex; instead we were open to any opportunity to have sex with people we knew. One favorite memory is Arthur and I fucking while a jazz musician friend played his upright bass at the foot of the bed. Of course the musician and I had sex next!

Someone once said to me that she thought sex was sacred and special only if it was within a committed relationship. She'd had sex outside of a committed relationship in the past; she said she had felt "degraded."

I told her that I don't think of it that way at all. I think of sex-outside-of-a-committed-relationship as a special link between me and another person. The first time I had sex with more than one person was before I met Arthur, with my college boyfriend and his best friend. It was the day I was leaving for the Soviet Union. The two men had obviously discussed it beforehand, and I was reluctant. But at a certain point I said "what the hell, it's a new experience!" My memory is hazy but sweet, the two of them loving on my body, and then the horrifying moment when I realized that I should have already left for the airport! So it ended very abruptly. I don't even know the man's name, I never saw him again, and was with him for a couple of hours total. But there is a special connection between he and I that goes far beyond what I would feel if we had just hung out in his apartment listening to music, etc. I probably wouldn't remember him at all in that case.

Degrading? Not at all. Many of these sexual experiences were, for me, fantastic expressions of what could be if we were liberated from our cultural beliefs about sex: moments of deep intimacy with friends or casual acquaintances. But it was really difficult to escape the subjective beliefs of everyone involved, me included, about what the sex *meant*. I eventually gave it up because it seemed too hard, but I have never lost the belief in the possibility of truly liberated sexuality.

❖

Many times Arthur has told me a quote he heard somewhere: "sex ain't dirty unless you do it right." I never could get my mind around this; the meaning always puzzled me because this statement completely went against my ideals about sex. My opinion is this is exactly what's *wrong* with sex: the reason we have so many problems with sex is precisely *because* we think it is dirty.

In *Masters of Sex*, a book about the sexual research team of Masters and Johnson, Thomas Maier writes, "So many patients had been taught that sex was wrong that it rendered them unable to make love in a mature or even adequate way." He quotes Virginia Johnson saying, "What is totally foreign to effective sexual development, in spite of centuries of practice, is the notion that sex is dirty, supplemented by various controls exercised through fear, rejection, ignorance, and misconception." [72]

"Sex is dirty" is another destructive subjective belief, a component of our culture's collective reality. It has harmed us all.

Another name I have for clean sex is "conscious sex." Conscious sex is clean because it's sex without lust. When I use the word "lust" I'm thinking of these dictionary definitions: "uncontrolled desire," or "overmastering desire," which I translate as "being driven by unconscious desires."

For must of us, sex happens when we feel desire, when we're aroused. We believe that you can't turn sex on like a light bulb, you can't make desire happen, and that sex without desire is never going to be hot. Sex needs lust.

Perhaps this is the meaning of "sex ain't dirty unless you do it right": take the twisted cultural belief that sex is naughty and run with it; exploit the energy embedded in the wrongness. This does give a thrill, but, I would suggest, it's limited.

I have discovered that conscious sex is something that you can initiate without being aroused. Sexual energy is always flowing, like all forms of life energy. You can open yourself up to tap into that energy flow at any time, and if you stay open you can ride the sexual energy wave into places of bliss, without need for exotic tricks to keep you interested. And, in my experience, conscious sex goes to far deeper and higher places than ordinary lust-driven sex ever took me; once I discovered it I never wanted to go back.

I think of it this way: when I want to have sex I shift my awareness to tap into the ocean of sexual energy, then I climb on my surfboard and get out on the leading edge and ride the wave wherever it goes. It's all about staying right there on the edge of the wave, not thinking about anything, just moving with the flow of energy.

Of course you can get hot when you follow the tried-and-true path of whatever sexual trip turns you on, but it only goes so deep. It's easy to get bored and feel the need to find new variations. Conscious sex is endlessly interesting because it is experienced in the present where every moment is new.

The concept of dirtiness comes from the subjective mind. When I'm having dirty sex I'm lost in my thoughts, filtering my experience through a thick layer of pre-conceptions that remove me from the here-and-now exquisiteness of my body. In dirty sex I'm telling stories about sex to myself, that is, I'm thinking. You could call it "unconscious sex," which involves things like make-believe sex games and fantasies. These are activities that keep the mind going—during an activity that is best when it is free of thought.

Not thinking is key: conscious sex happens in the present moment. Thinking takes me away to some abstract idea, or memory of the past, or imaginary role. I'm not here and now with what's happening, I'm in some thought-realm adding a spin to whatever's happening.

After many years of being in a committed relationship sex can get stale. Sex experts advise us that the answer is to spice up our marriage with something new. Buy some sexy lingerie or start playing games, like "country gentleman and his French maid." The thinking is that you've exhausted all the possibilities; I sucked that same cock for so many years what could I possibly do that I haven't done before? But the truth is this moment of now is always different and new, and this moment of sexual energy is always different and new. I may have sucked that same cock a thousand times before, but I never sucked it in *this* moment of now before!

I mentioned before that Arthur and I would often find a new sexual position when we had sex after resolving an argument. Telling the truth about an issue would temporarily break up our patterns of relating, leaving an open space, and in that openness we could find newness within movements we had made hundreds of times before.

I think that for most people, myself included, sex is the time when they are most free of the tyranny of the mind. That is part of its wonder for us; for a few moments we can experience the bliss of an alternate reality. But in my experience, even though you might stop having thoughts like, "don't forget to put the clothes in the dryer," the mind is still pumping out thoughts: "his ass looks good," "turn this way so I can see us better in the mirror," "I hope someone is watching us through the window," "wow this feels amazing," etc.

Being here now when I fuck means I let go of *all* thinking, being in the present as fully as possible. The most amazing thing I have experienced when I do this is that my body moves in the perfect way to increase my pleasure; and this movement is completely outside of any conscious control. It is like I am allowing my body to take charge of the fuck, without my (that is, my subjective mind's) ideas of how to help.

Just recently I had an experience where it felt like I was being moved by a force emanating from my navel—anyone familiar with Carlos Castaneda will remember Don Juan's description of this as the place where energy radiates from the body. I let go of any conscious control of my body's movement and allowed myself to be pulled by this tether and it led to the most amazing places of sexual connection with Arthur. It was like I was tethered to the sexual energy force and my entire body moved without any resistance to the flow.

In clean sex I feel like I am a teen-ager who was never told anything about sex, and I met another teen-ager who also was never told anything about sex, and we followed the feelings of our bodies to do that which created the most exquisite sensations. Communication flowing between us so fully that touching him is touching myself. Pure and clean.

Note to myself: The strength of the "O" is reflected in the length of the glow.

19

Completion

In Alcoholics Anonymous, the tough but experienced advice for those wanting to help an unrepentant drinker face his or her alcoholism is to buy them a bottle! The idea is to assist the drinker in *hitting bottom*. The moment of hitting bottom is the crucial point at which the drinker at last faces the objective truth of his or her addiction. AA calls this *the turning point*. The lie the alcoholic's subjective mind has been telling, "I can handle alcohol," is fully exposed, loses its power, and begins to die.

In the same way, it makes sense for us to encourage subjective mind to reach its peak of madness, because when we understand its destructive power we are emboldened to question our Story.

Self-destructive behavior patterns like alcoholism survive by convincing us that they make us happy when the objective truth is that they cause us pain. When we discover the painful nature of a behavior we consider abandoning it. But part of us (the network of beliefs that form the "this behavior = happiness" filter) still clings to the happiness illusion. Thus, when we think about giving the behavior up, our subjective mind tells us we are losing something of value. This is why we often feel deprived or threatened when we consider changing a behavior pattern.

In addition, remember a thought-form's survival strategy: when we have identified with a behavior pattern, we feel like its death means *our* death.

As long as we believe we're *losing* when we abandon a behavior or belief, we will never truly be free of it. The turning point of any self-destructive behavior comes when we experience that we're not losing by giving the behavior up—we're *gaining*.

Arthur calls this the "one last steak" syndrome. I was a very committed vegetarian for over twenty years. Arthur was intellectually persuaded that vegetarianism was right, but he struggled with a deeply embedded desire for meat. Whenever he thought he was going to commit to vegetarianism he would start lobbying for "just one last steak": a one-pound, medium-rare, New York strip to see him on his way. In Arthur's words, the steak's "juicy flavors would linger in my memory down the long and dismal years of vegetarian deprivation." Of course, with this attitude, that "one last steak" was never the last! When Arthur got depressed or angry he'd visit our local meat market and tell the grinning butcher as he bellied up to the case, "I fell off the meat wagon again!"

And notice Arthur's feelings of depression and anger: the subjective mind often creates an emotional crisis as justification for a return to a behavior that we have quit—"this situation is too stressful to bear without a cigarette," "I've had a difficult day so I deserve a bucket of ice cream," etc. Of course at the time we think the crisis is real and are unaware that it was created by our subjective mind as an excuse to feed our addiction.

I've heard alcoholics say that they were actually grateful for being drunks. They had a clear, dysfunctional behavior pattern that painfully forced them into the experience of humility and spirituality. Jesus is reported to have said, "Blessed are the poor in spirit, for theirs is the kingdom of heaven." From this statement one could infer, "Cursed are the reasonable in spirit, those who play life by all the rules, conform, keep their mouths shut and do what they're told, those who imagine themselves somehow to be normal through and through, and without any major problems...for theirs is the kingdom of hell: the utter self-delusion of the subjective-mind slave."

Another Zen story tells about two monks who come to a flooded stream and find a beautiful young woman trying to find a way to cross it. One of the monks offers to carry her across on his back and she gratefully accepts. He carries her over, she thanks him, and the two monks continue on their way. After a while, the monk who did not carry the woman begins to scold the other, reminding him that such close physical contact with a female is frowned upon—even forbidden—by their order. He continues in this manner until the monk who carried the woman replies, "I put the woman down when we reached the other side of the stream. Are you still carrying her?"[73]

You can't leave something behind until you're *complete* with it, until you are objectively aware that your indulgences, desires, appetites, addictions, and lusts do not produce happiness, love, or satisfaction.

The centered monk could feel—without becoming aroused—a young female body glued to his back for the duration of the river crossing, and then put her down and think no more about her. He could do this only because he was in no way excited or titillated by the woman's body. He was complete with his sexuality. He had no unfaced or unacknowledged sexual desires, which such an intimate experience could bring to the surface to surprise and control him. The other monk, however, clearly had some incompletion in the area of sex. He became agitated and thrown off balance by his own incomplete sexuality; he became disturbed (righteous moral indignation concealing envy and desire) by watching his companion carry the young woman.

A.A. literature is full of stories of alcoholics, sober for twenty years, who had a sudden and overwhelming urge to drink that took them totally by surprise and against which they were utterly powerless. These unfortunate people were not complete with their desire for alcohol.

Many of us think the best way to handle an addiction or desire is to suppress it—to cram the thing into our subconscious. But because it is still an incomplete issue it has the potential to erupt at a future time.

❖

"Complete" [*Webster's*]: *having all parts or elements; lacking nothing; whole; entire; full.* Synonyms for "complete" are intact; perfect; absolute; thorough; undivided; unity; integrity.

Every moment of reality has all parts or elements, lacks nothing, and is whole, entire, full, and complete. Reality is *always* complete. Reality is *always* perfect. If we are unhappy with any given moment of now it is because we are subjectively value-judging it as "lacking" in something, as "incomplete."

Subjective mind is able to convince us that a negative or self-destructive behavior pattern is good for us because it never permits us to objectively observe all the information available to us about the behavior: the consequences, the rewards, the price, the results. To quote the above definition, we are never permitted to see "all parts, all elements." We cannot see the big picture. We are only allowed to see the part of the picture that justifies our continued indulgence. We are only permitted to see that information which supports the survival of the behavior-rationalizing beliefs.

You could say Arthur was "incomplete with meat" and that's why he couldn't become a vegetarian; something would be missing whenever he had a meal.

Being incomplete is like being in debt. As long as we owe something we're not free; there are obligations that must be met. Incompletion is a form of obligation—something is required of us. When we feel incomplete with another it means that something that needs to be said or done hasn't been said or done. As long as this is true, whenever we think of that person or are around them we will always feel like something is missing, something needs to happen.

Much of the grief displayed at death, expressed by both the dying and the surviving, arises from the horror of being incomplete when it's too late to do anything about it. True completion with another is only realized in the experience of love. This is simply because love, the experience of unconditional acceptance of what is, is the only state in which a person is perceived to be perfect just the way they are.

I have integrated these ideas into another phrase: *honest indulgence to completion.*

Honest indulgence to completion means that I drop all pretense of struggling to give up a self-destructive behavior or thought pattern when the truth is I'm still clinging to it and, as objectively and honestly as possible, observe the pattern in operation. Either the pattern is running my life or it isn't. If it is, watch it, let it do its thing, and try to tell the truth about what I see. Don't beat myself up for behaving or thinking that way. Realize that I'm insane and confused. Just watch and question. Does the behavior or thought produce love or hate, happiness or suffering? Indulging in shame, denial, and/or fruitless struggle against a power I don't understand doesn't accomplish anything. Until I'm complete my struggle is a sham and a further excuse to despise myself whenever I indulge. The guilt I wallow in when I fail is, in fact, the price I willingly pay in order to justify my continued indulgence in a behavior or thought.

❖

A "self-destructive behavior pattern" doesn't mean just drinking excessively or eating compulsively. Self-destructive (insane) behavior arises from the entrenched subjective beliefs that cause us to follow the fixed plot lines of My Story for a lifetime. "I am not attractive" is an addictive and self-destructive thought pattern that leads to patterns of behavior with innumerable negative consequences.

The word "honest" is very important in "honest indulgence to completion." I'm not talking about mindless indulgence (although A.A. tells us that *can* lead to the turning point), but rather a conscious witnessing of my behavior and its results. Honesty can take us from unconscious suppression to completion.

This formula works for any behavior pattern. For example, I have always hated waiting in line. When I found myself in a long line, or a checkout person was slow, impatience would wash over me and I would get angry. (One of my favorite parts of living in a small town was I almost never had to wait anywhere—bank, post office, grocery store, etc.) I hated myself for this lack of patience, because it seemed like it was a complete rejection of everything I have learned about acceptance!

I began a routine where every evening I would mentally go back over my day, assessing my behavior towards other people (and this also included time on the phone with customer service representatives and telemarketers). Did I feel impatience or anger? Was I rude? Was I even just a little grumpy?

After some time of doing this, I was aware enough that in the moment, when I saw that I was going to have to wait in line, I could watch myself and monitor the irritation. By doing that I could release it. I still feel the irritation, but I am more and more successful at preventing the anger and rudeness. Maybe one day soon I'll be complete with my impatience with lines.

This illustrates a point I made earlier: my emotions and behavior are an excellent guide to what is in my mind. My subjective mind can be very slippery about what I *really* think and feel. I believe I'm a nice person, so My Story doesn't include that I'm rude to strangers for no better reason than I think I'm too important to wait in line. So I'll come up with all sorts of rationalizations for why I'm acting like a jerk.

But when I take responsibility for my actions and emotions, I say, "If I'm behaving like a jerk it's because of my attitude, not the external circumstance. There's some reason—I may not know what it is, but that's not important now. What is important is that it's not producing the results I want (I don't want to be a jerk). What I do know is my behavior shows I'm not accepting reality as it is right now." By going through this process I can at least apply the brakes to whatever negative action or emotion I'm feeling.

❖

My "pathless path" is simply the experience of surrender (which is acceptance) to what is (which is reality). Accept reality. Allow reality to be the way it already is and move toward sanity.

When it's raining, accept that it's raining. Maybe it spoiled my plans to go on a hike, but that was just an image of the future I had created in my mind—let it go. When I'm depressed, accept that I'm depressed. If I think I should always be happy that's a delusional expectation in a dualistic universe. When I've cut my hand, accept that I've hurt myself. Be cool. Accept the way it already is. When my train of awareness (always several seconds late) chugs into the station of Here and Now, just look around and accept what I find there. This is comparative sanity.

And: When the roof leaks, accept that it's leaking and fix it, unless the water on the floor doesn't matter. The pathless path doesn't mean that I do nothing. I take care of business, get my teeth cleaned, pay the bills, and do the best I can: recognizing that I am *always* doing my best in every moment. When I've cut my hand, I see a doctor. And, when I lose my cool and get angry, I accept that I'm rejecting reality—I'm nuts!—and I question the Story that rationalized the crazy behavior.

My pathless path could be summed up in this saying attributed to Buddha: "Act always as if the future of the universe depended on what you did, while laughing at yourself for thinking that whatever you do makes any difference." There is never anything to be proud of. There is never anything to feel superior about. There is never anything to be ashamed of or feel inferior about.

The pathless path says: admit my limitations, experience humility, question My Story, bend like a willow to the way it is, and be honest about the cost of blindly following the dictates of my subjective-mind tyrant.

So how do I know whether I'm being subjective or objective? If the subjective mind is such a master controller that the human race has been its unconscious slave for all of recorded history, what chance do I have of knowing who's in the driver's seat at any given moment? Once again: check the results of my behavior. Jesus said, "By their fruits you will know them." What are the fruits of my words and actions?

Am I anxious, irritated, mean, frustrated, bored, depressed, angry, sad, hating, lonely, or condescending? Then it's obvious: subjective mind is in the driver's seat.

Indicators of Insanity:

No experience of love.

Loneliness, no true intimacy, separate, isolated, no one we can "really talk to."

Violence, hatred, anger, irritation, mild displeasure.

Dissatisfaction, perceiving imperfection, unhappiness, restlessness, boredom.

Blaming anyone or anything, guilt, shame.

Fear, uncertainty, insecurity, worry, anxiety, depression.

Pride, arrogance, competition, envy, taking oneself too seriously.

Elitism, sexism, racism, anythingthatdrawsalineism.

Gossip, feeling good at another's failure or shortcomings.

Addiction, compulsion, obsession, lust, greed, selfishness.

Regret and remorse for the past, anxiety about the future, longing for an ideal future, hope.

Lying, exaggerating, boasting.

Feeling of inferiority or superiority.

Indicators of (Relative) Sanity:

The experience of love.

Full self-expression, honest, truthful.

Fulfillment and satisfaction, absence of desire and fear, secure.

Non-violent, non-aggressive, peaceful.

Compassionate, understanding, willing to listen to and accept others' realities.

Open-minded, curious, willing to learn and change, creative, inventive, inspired.

Gratitude.

Humble, willingness to acknowledge mistakes, able to laugh at oneself.

Being here now, accepting the perfection of the present and all past moments.

Caring, giving, generous to everyone and everything.

Aware of the perfection and interconnectedness of all things.

Centered, serene, unemotional.

Feeling of equality.

20

The Mechanics of Compassion

At the end of the last chapter I listed compassion—not forgiveness—as an indicator of (relative) sanity. By relative sanity I mean not confusing my subjective opinions with objective fact.

Compassion: *the experience that arises from the perception of the limitations of another or one's self without value judgment.*

Compassion understands the limitations imposed by insanity and physicality. Compassion sees that because delusional insanity is universal, and all our thoughts and actions proceed from delusional insanity, no one freely chooses to do wrong. Compassion sees that everyone suffers, because everyone is limited. Compassion sees objective reality undistorted by subjective value judgment.

Compassion is not forgiveness. The concept of forgiveness is based on the belief in free will: a deliberate wrong was committed which needs to be forgiven or apologized for.

Compassion sees that no forgiveness is, or ever has been, necessary because there is no such thing as free will. One does not stroll the wards of a mental hospital forgiving the patients for their behavior; we understand that their actions come from their mental illness. In the same way, if we accept universal human insanity, we understand that people's behavior, no matter how horrible, proceeds from their mental confusion.

Webster's defines "forgive": *to give up resentment against or the desire to punish; stop being angry with; pardon.*

Forgiveness can actually be used as another weapon in the subjective mind's arsenal.

When we say, "I forgive you," we like to believe that the incident is thereby settled; all over and done with; forgotten. However, as the *Webster's* definition makes clear, forgiveness does not mean forgetting the wrong, it means letting go of anger at the wrongdoer and letting go of the desire for retribution for the wrongdoing. The belief that a wrong has been deliberately committed is in no way altered—much less forgotten—by the act of forgiveness. I have heard more than one person say, "I forgive...but I never forget." This makes the point perfectly. In the realm of subjective mind, there is no forgetting. The subjective mind remembers every "wrong" and uses it to its advantage.

Henry Ward Beecher, an extremely popular American clergyman in the mid-1800s (brother of author Harriet Beecher Stowe), understood this basic flaw in the concept of forgiveness. He wrote, "'I can forgive, but I cannot forget,' is only another way of saying, 'I will not forgive.' Forgiveness ought to be like a cancelled note—torn in two, and burned up, so that it never can be shown against one."[74]

How many of us have experienced this scenario: Someone commits what we thinks is a willful wrongdoing and at some point we say with what we believe to be sincerity, "I forgive you." We now assume that this incident is over and done with. Then, at some future date, we get angry at that person about something else. Suddenly up pops the "forgiven" act and we seize upon it as further justification for our anger about the current situation: "Remember the time you _____, you asshole!!!"

The surprising way in which supposedly forgiven ancient history resurfaces in arguments demonstrates that our original conviction, that the person was *guilty*, remains fixed and unchanged through time, our "forgiveness" notwithstanding. This is tantamount to having a criminal record. You have served your time in prison and have paid your debt to society. However, the stigma of the crime remains, and you are never truly forgiven. You will always be eyed with suspicion because you were guilty—you did what you did *on purpose*, you *freely chose* your crime, your character is obviously flawed, and you can never be trusted again.

The permanent denial of a felon's right to vote in a number of states is an example of this thinking. A felon's right to full citizenship has been forever revoked. The felon remains branded and penalized for the rest of his or her life.

In contrast, compassion doesn't forget a wrong because compassion never sees a wrong in the first place (in the sense of free-will-chosen wrongdoing). Compassion, like acceptance, is not blind—compassion remembers all the facts of a particular event, but does not label them "wrong," or the perpetrator (eminently including one's self) "guilty" and "flawed." Compassion does not harbor value judgments about past events. When compassion is present, reality is perceived accurately; therefore one is complete with it and can let it go.

❖

The very word "forgiveness" clearly includes the idea of "giving." When a person says the words "I forgive you," what is really being said is "I am *giving* you my forgiveness, I am *bestowing* my pardon upon you, I am *offering* you another chance," etc. What this means is that the forgiver enjoys a position clearly superior to that of the forgiven. When you give something to another, you place that person in your debt: there is an unspoken demand or expectation for reciprocity, whether consciously realized or not. Reciprocity can mean either a return gift of equal value, or a suitable display of humble gratitude. The subjective mind is willing, indeed eager, to say the words "I forgive you," because forgiving is a magnanimous act that puts the subjective mind in its favorite place: on top.

As children, most of us were trained to beg forgiveness whether we meant it or not. When we broke the cookie jar we learned to whine, "I'm sorry," because we had already learned that this was the surest way to minimize parental wrath and retribution. The truth is, if we were sincerely "sorry" about anything it was for being caught (sorry the cookie jar broke and made our cookie-stealing impossible to conceal). On top of that, most of us never truly accepted the rule, Thou Shalt Not Eat Cookies Except When Dispensed By Adults, and, because we saw this rule as being arbitrarily and unfairly imposed upon us, we didn't see the breaking of the rule to be a wrong requiring forgiveness.

Once we learned to mouth the magic words "I'm sorry" (a declaration of self-worthlessness), we employed them even when we were accused of wrongs that were beyond our comprehension.

A toddler discovers Daddy's *Playboy* collection and is having the time of her life examining the strange and fascinating photographs when she finds herself being screamed at by a deranged-acting parent. Even though she has no idea what her offense is, out comes the verbal talisman that has the magical ability to soothe the savage parent. What we learn as children is that groveling, self-abasement, and insincerity are all pro-survival tools. The precedent for this deferential behavior is found throughout the animal kingdom in those rituals that establish and maintain pecking orders within social groups.

Webster's defines "apology" as: *an acknowledgment of some fault, injury, insult, wrong, etc., with an expression of regret and a plea for pardon.*

Is apology ever appropriate? If one believes in free will the answer would have to be yes, because the person asking your pardon is literally acknowledging his or her willful harm to you; stating that he or she freely and deliberately chose a course of action which was injurious to you. If free will were fact rather than fiction, apologies (and forgiveness) would indeed be in order.

You bump someone's shoulder in the hallway and out pops "Oh! Excuse me!" or, "I beg your pardon!" Why? The better to survive, that's why. Failure to mouth the words of contrition might lead to anger on the bumped person's part, which is an anti-survival situation (anger potentially leads to violence which potentially leads to death). This type of apology is as automatic and meaningless as the "Hi, how are you?" "Fine, thanks, how are you?" exchange. Etiquette is a code of tribal survival behavior. Mouthing the correct clichés, like using the correct fork at table, establishes trust that one is a tribal member-in-good-standing, and is thus less likely to attack.

Apology proclaims that a certain behavior is wrong. If the apology is sincere, then obviously we should never repeat that behavior again. Duh! The reason that we often find ourselves apologizing again and again for the identical behavior shows that our apologies were superficial in nature and not truly sincere. To sincerely acknowledge that a behavior is wrong is to disavow the beliefs that direct it. This is a direct survival threat to those beliefs and the subjective mind will fiercely defend against it.

The subjective mind utilizes apology to deflect attention away from the belief or beliefs that motivated or directed the offensive behavior. It does this in order to prevent any real questioning of the beliefs' structural integrity or truthfulness. Apology is often a subterfuge, an imitation of good-heartedness, and an obsequious false humility that merely poses as sincerity in order for subjective mind to survive unchanged.

In my submissive role in my relationship with Arthur I would often say, "I'm sorry Arthur," to end an argument, even if I didn't think I was wrong. I had been raised by two people who never argued in front of the children (until the day Dad up and left) and in My Story arguing was a bad thing that needed to be avoided at all costs. One day Arthur's daughter, when she was still a young child, said to me, "Don't say you're sorry, Katie. It's not true." She could see that I was lying, but I was powerless at that time to change. Her words stuck with me though, and I have mostly quit saying it.

When I first started holding to my position in a discussion or argument, Arthur accused me of getting hard and tough. He was so used to getting his way that it was a shock when I resisted. But what had become clear to me was that when I had said "I'm sorry" to end arguments I still believed I was right, so I would be seething with resentment inside even while I superficially acted as if the argument was over. Obviously there could never be a true resolution of the problem as long as I felt this way, just a band-aid covering it up.

Note to myself: Crazy means *never* having to say you're sorry. That doesn't mean I don't say, "I was/am incorrect" or "I realize I hurt you." It doesn't mean I don't stop and question why I did something that hurt another.

❖

We have all been indoctrinated into the belief-system of forgiveness and apology. Forgiveness and apology are socially mandated behaviors that have superficially maintained a certain degree of tribal order. Forgiveness and apology grease the wheels of human interaction.

Compassion sees reality as perfect the way it is; free from wrong; a flawless and inevitable manifestation of universal forces; the Big Bang after almost fourteen billion years of processing. It's absurd to say to a volcano, "I *forgive* you for the eruption." It's equally absurd to say to the mugger who assaulted you for the contents of your wallet, "I *forgive* you for mugging me."

Forgiveness would say to the mugger, "You had a choice and you made a wrong choice. I am willing to forgive you for making that wrong choice, but it is literally impossible for me to ever forget that you willfully chose to do wrong. You need to be punished for your willful choice."

Compassion would say to the mugger, "You were compelled to take a course of action that your beliefs convinced you was pro-survival and justified. You are insane; you are in a state of severe delusion and confusion, you are obviously powerless over your false beliefs which are destructive to yourself and others, and you must get help because the stability of society insists upon it." This is the behavior of a so-called saint; someone I would say is relatively sane. Compassion is not some lofty head-in-the-clouds idealism. It is feet-on-the-ground practicality. Compassion is not weak. It is powerful.

Today, forgiveness is often prescribed as a therapeutic treatment. When one forgives one's childhood abuser, for example, one does so to be set free, to no longer be under the control of the abuser, to no longer be affected by the trauma of the abuse, to no longer carry the burden of hatred and shame. To experience real therapeutic results, however, compassion is required. The superficial ritual of forgiveness leaves in place the fatal belief that the offense was committed deliberately by an evil person.

The only way to be truly free is to see that no forgiveness is, or ever has been, necessary—that the abuser in question had absolutely no choice but to behave as he or she did and is innocent by reason of insanity. One may know one has attained compassion when one literally experiences love for—in this example—one's childhood abuser. No matter how great the injury, the moment that a sufficiently accurate and objective perception of reality has been achieved—the person inflicting the injury was literally insane—compassion and love for that person will follow.

Compassion is selfless. It is said that when Jesus was being crucified, he was not focusing on the injury being done to him; he was saying, "Forgive them, *for they know not what they do.*" Jesus knew that, just as the volcano "knows not what it does" when it blows its stack, no forgiveness (even for one's murderers) is ever required. Even though the word "forgiveness" is regularly used in the gospels, it is clear that what Jesus preached was compassion: "Let he who is without guilt cast the first stone."

I'll anticipate the inevitable charge that all of this is merely bleeding heart naiveté. Some would argue that what is being presented here is some sort of weepy, sentimental, and overly-sympathetic perception of lawbreakers which would allow them to literally get away with murder because "it's not their fault, they were poor, they were abused, they didn't know what they were doing, etc." Yet if someone does not know what they are doing (even while thinking they do), how could they possibly be blamed for their behavior? Only someone who is deeply attached to the belief in free will and revenge could find such a person blameworthy.

Refraining from blame doesn't mean not taking action to remove a lawbreaker from society. We would continue to put killers, pedophiles, rapists, etc. in prison (until we gain enough compassion to build secure mental hospitals), we just wouldn't label them "evil." We'd also take steps to eliminate the causes of crime, such as poverty, ignorance, social isolation, and mental illness (in the conventional meaning).

Compassion sees the absolute perfection of the universe. Compassion understands that there are no mistakes possible in a perfect universe. Compassion perceives the mitigating factors and extenuating circumstances that inevitably lead to an event or action. Compassion sees that human beings under the spell of delusional insanity will do crazy things.

Compassion sees that everything is, and always has been, and always will be, perfect. Perfect here means "whole and complete."

Reality is what is.

Reality is perfect. The here and now is whole and complete.

Acceptance is the objective perception of the perfection of what is.

Love, sanity, and compassion are identical states of awareness: the experience of unconditional acceptance of what is.

Compassion is acceptance. Compassion is love. Compassion is sanity.

Without compassion there is only madness, the terrible delusion that existent reality could or should be some other way and that we do evil to others and ourselves deliberately.

Compassion sees that never under any circumstance or at any

time is there any basis for hating ourselves or another.

❖

To illustrate how compassion works, think of someone you are angry with, and bring to mind a specific incident or trait that you believe justifies your anger. Find an example that seems to be a perfect illustration of a willful wrongdoing or shortcoming on this person's part.

Now take a step back and attempt to objectively apply some of the principles in this book. In the following exercise, insert the person's name in the single underline space, and a brief repeatable phrase describing the person's specific wrongdoing or shortcoming in the bold underline space (for example, <u>Bill</u> makes me angry because he/she **gossiped about me**):

_____ makes me angry because he/she _____.

I am angry because I believe that _____ _____ on purpose.

I can see that _____'s behavior is fully justified in his/her mind by his/her beliefs.

I can see that _____'s beliefs compelled him/her to _____because he/she is convinced that his/her justifications are true; are reality.

I can see that _____ doesn't think that he/she is wrong for _____ because _____ has effectively rationalized his/her behavior and beliefs.

I can see that _____ may not even believe he/she _____.

I can see that _____ is not evil, _____ is confused; is driven by false beliefs; is insane.

I can experience compassion for _____ because I see that _____ is innocent by reason of insanity.

I can see that _____ has served me. The very fact that I am angry indicates that I am reacting defensively and irrationally; therefore I am insecure in myself.

I can see that being angry with an insane person is equally insane.

I can see that taking an insane person's actions personally is insane.

I can see that my subjective mind may be preventing me from seeing reality objectively and the wrongdoing or shortcoming I am ascribing to _____ might be partially or entirely a delusion that doesn't exist in objective reality.

I can experience compassion for myself for being angry at _____, because, as an insane person, I am also innocent.

Steps one and two are the classic foundational arguments upon which subjective mind builds its case for blame, anger, and retaliation. Steps one and two cry, "You molested my child and I hate you for it!" The following steps transcend hatred and emotion by objectively perceiving reality. "You are a pedophile, a deeply disturbed person at the mercy of distorted values which manifest as uncontrollable sexual attraction for children. I can see why your deranged sexual beliefs drove you to molest my child; I have compassion for you as the helpless victim of a twisted mental state. I further understand that any fear, hatred, blame, or shame on my part—however understandable—arises from my own insanity, my own inability to see objectively."

These steps are the mechanics of compassion.

Compassion may also say, "I see that this pedophile is a threat to others and must be forcibly removed from society and treated." But because of compassion there will be treatment rather than punishment; the goal is to cure a person afflicted by a terrible mental illness.

There is never any sane justification for being angry at any one or at any thing at any time in any place for any reason.

Another word for angry is "mad." "Mad" is also a common synonym of "insane." As anger is a clear manifestation of insanity, "getting mad" seems an entirely appropriate descriptive.

The single cause of all evil, sin, wrongdoing, mischief, rudeness, malice, cruelty, crime, violence, and war is insanity. To become angry with an insane person, to blame and/or shame them for their insane behavior, is also insane. Most of us are entirely oblivious to this because *we* are insane, and thus we blame others and ourselves on a daily basis. Most of us have been programmed to use blame and shame just like all of the other inmates in our planetary lunatic asylum.

Martin Luther King, Jr. embodied the principles of compassion outlined above. In *Stride Toward Freedom,* his account of the Montgomery, Alabama bus boycott (1955-6), he wrote about his thoughts the night his house was bombed. He had compassion for the white people involved because he realized that they had been taught to think that black people were inferior; they were good people who did bad things because of their cultural conditioning.[75]

Dr. King was a powerful leader because of his compassion—he motivated millions of people to confront our country's legacy of hatred and bigotry not with anger but with peaceful, non-violent action. Through this enlightened attitude he brought about significant progress in civil rights.

The mechanics of compassion are:

Accept our insanity. We are deluded about reality and, as a result, are limited in our understanding of everything.

Experience humility. Humility naturally follows the realization of our insanity. In the state of humility we recognize and accept our limitations.

Observe without value judgment. Because we no longer have to deny and defend our limitations, we are free to extend the same courtesy to others: we can perceive their limitations without value-judging them, and understand that they, like us, are driven to do the things they do by delusional insanity.

Experience compassion.

21

Love is Sanity

Most of us are so love-starved we find it inconceivable that love could be our normal operating system of awareness.

Love is not something that can be chopped up into different categories: family love, romantic love, brotherly/sisterly love, puppy love, love of country, love of work, love of chili dogs. Love is not something to be reserved for the special people in your life.

Love is the experience of unconditional acceptance of what is. This means that love is a state of awareness: when we accept existent reality, we experience love.

Acceptance of reality doesn't mean we are incapable of perceiving that existent reality *could* be other than it is—at some future point. We can plan to build a bridge, but we are insane to hate the unbridged river. Reality is what is, and is—at the moment of perception—an immutable fact that is either sanely accepted or insanely rejected.

"Unconditional acceptance" means no rules, no limits, and no boundaries to our experience of the perfection of what is. It means there's no condition that we impose before we say, "This is acceptable."

But to be able to accept without conditions means we must know what it is we're trying to accept. I can't accept something I'm not aware of. For example, I can't accept what is hidden from me behind a curtain because I don't know what's back there. Maybe it's my worst nightmare! Our capacity to love is, therefore, limited by our capacity to know.

Most of us experience love for only a few people because of our subjective beliefs about reality. If we could drop our allegiance to subjective mind we could begin to experience love for more and more people, ultimately for all people, and for all things. Because we don't have to possess the object of our love, or do anything about it except enjoy the experience of love, we would be free to feel acceptance/love towards anyone.

I mentioned Arthur's song "Because I Love You" earlier; here are the lyrics:

> Because I love you doesn't mean I have to touch your hand
> Or look into your eyes and try to make you understand
> Because I love you doesn't take some word that's bound to try
> And capture this wild moment instead of letting it flow by
>
> Because I love you doesn't mean I have to let you know
> If anything it really means I have to let you go
> Because I love you as you are this instant you are free
> From all those crazy expectations, all the things I want to be
>
> The zoo is filled with good intentions
> Come see your beauty through the bars
> And wonder why your heart lacks all the tension
> That comes from the sight of a deer on the trail ahead
> Or the growl in the night when the campfire's dead
> And you feel your place with all beneath the stars
>
> Because I love you doesn't mean that I'm too blind to see
> That holding on to love is such a hopeless fantasy
> Because I love you doesn't mean we have to meet again
> So pass on stranger, go in peace, this love can never end

Love is the state of awareness that perceives what is as perfect, as intrinsically worthy, as deserving of respect and acceptance, with no preconceived notions that it *should* be any other way than the way it is right now.

To rephrase the definition of love: love is the perception of the perfection of what is.

Accepting reality exactly the way it is and exactly the way it is not is sanity. Love accepts what is, what was, and what will be. Love is sanity.

Being in a state of acceptance doesn't mean that we don't plan for the future, or fail to make our house payments and let the rain fall on our homeless heads. What it does mean is that we don't wait for tomorrow to be happy, to be at peace, or to be satisfied. We don't need anything more than what we have right now in order to have love, fulfillment, and peace. We don't need a new job, or a new life, or a new partner, or more money, or cosmetic surgery to be content.

When Arthur and I lived in San Francisco together in the early 1980's, we rode the California Street bus regularly. There was a lovely young woman who we often had the good fortune to have as a driver. She had long, blond hair that she always wore in a single braid down her back and a smiling personality that was beyond belief. She drove that bus as if she were driving a choir of angels to sing for God. Her bus never jerked or lurched, not an easy feat on the hills of San Francisco. Her passengers were often smiling and you could feel the positive effect that her attention to her driving had on all of us. She has always been a shining example to me of how transformation can look: you can be of genuine service and a real force for good wherever you find yourself.

❖

What would life be like without the domination of subjective mind?

Would we stop value judging? It's pleasant to imagine life without "bad" and "inferior" and "ugly," but what about life without "good" and "superior" and "beautiful"? When I walk in the woods, would I no longer appreciate the beauty of nature? Would I no longer perceive the magnificence of a piece of art or music? These disturbing questions have the happiest answer: the demotion of subjective mind to its proper place will not eliminate our experience of beauty but expand it.

First, as I said in the chapters on value, I'm not suggesting the abandonment of value judgment. I can still perceive the beauty in a work of art—I just no longer believe my appreciation *means* anything.

Second, in the state of acceptance we see everything as perfect, so we can see beauty and magnificence everywhere: the dirt at our feet, a rotting dead dog in a ditch, the faces of people twisted with rage or sadness. Beauty is in the eye of the beholder and if your eye is accepting there is no place where beauty is lacking. Perfection is always beautiful.

Our relationships with other people would also be transformed. We would no longer strive to attain power or pity (pity is another form of power); we would not manipulate interactions for our gain; we would not value-judge the worthiness of others. Christopher Isherwood, in *My Guru and I*, says that people who met his guru, Swami Prabhavananda, all used strikingly similar language to express their experience, something like: "you could see him more clearly, because he didn't have a personality getting in the way."[76]

A person who has transcended subjective-mind domination no longer has anything to prove. That is, she no longer has to defend and justify her subjective beliefs. As a result, she doesn't demand agreement or recognition, doesn't insist on being abused or loved, can't be hurt or let down. This is detachment, but that doesn't mean an anti-social or unfeeling attitude.

This is the type of individual you want to be around because they don't ask anything of you. Who you are is okay with them. You feel safe; because they are self-sufficient you can trust them.

A mantra of mine:

> I don't need anyone.
> I don't need anything.
> I don't need anything from anyone.
> I already have everything I need.
> In fact I have an abundance to give.

This doesn't mean I don't recognize my absolute interdependence with everyone. Recognizing my limitations has actually made it much easier for me to ask for help, and to say "yes" to offers of help even when I don't think I need it. What this mantra means to me is that I don't need another person to complete me.

In the past, when I would talk to someone part of my communication always had a "please like me" aspect to it. There was a pleading in my eyes: "please understand me." My Story said, "I'm shy and I'm better than egotistical extroverts because they dominate social gatherings." But then one day I realized that shy people like me were dominating in another way: I expected other people to make more of an effort to talk to me. I needed help *because* I was shy.

They had to come up to me and initiate the conversation. This is the kind of neediness I am referring to in the mantra.

❖

Another benefit of the downgrading of subjective mind is no longer agonizing over decisions or wallowing in regret. As we've seen, although it appears as though we are constantly confronted with choices, our unconscious psychological processes always make one "choice" inevitable—and thus no choice at all. While reality forces us to *act* as though we are choosing, we must keep in mind that no true choice is involved. We do not have free will.

Recently a friend described to me the turmoil she was experiencing while trying to make a major life decision. As I listened it occurred to me that the reason it is often difficult to make decisions is because we believe that down one path lies happiness, and down the other unhappiness. We become paralyzed by the fear of choosing the wrong path and ending up unhappy. The truth is that happiness does not depend on the circumstances. Whether we are happy or not is completely determined by our state of awareness. Happiness is a byproduct of acceptance. The more we accept the way it is right now, without subjective value judgments piled on top of our objective perception, the happier we are.

No matter which path we end up taking, we will be happy or unhappy exactly to the extent that we are in a state of acceptance. So my advice to my friend was: "what you choose will not make any difference as to your happiness, so make the choice based on what seems to be the best action given the information you now have."

At the end of the film *Zorba the Greek,* the inhibited Englishman, who had seemed incapable of being happy no matter the circumstance, lost everything in the catastrophic failure of his mining venture. At that moment he asked Zorba to teach him to dance. To dance in the midst of ruin is to transcend ruin.[77]

❖

We are all insane. Recognizing that we are confused is the way out. Being humble about our limitations is the way to open up our awareness. Questioning our beliefs helps us attain comparative sanity.

We are all innocent by reason of insanity.

As you may recall, "innocent" has two meanings. The first is "not guilty": when we recognize our insanity we realize that we are *innocent* of all the charges we have levied against ourselves.

The other meaning of innocent is "virtuous, flawless, without sin or moral wrong." This is what I called *innocence*: we are without sin by reason of insanity.

Innocence means to be filled with wonder, curiosity, and awe at the marvelous perfection and ever-changing complexity of the mystery of existence. The opposite of innocence is the jaded adult cynicism most of us are all too familiar with; life on autopilot, steeped in boredom, routine, and faked enthusiasm; the rigidity of the subjective-belief slave.

Innocence means to be liberated from our false imitations of knowledge, from the fatal presumption that we know anything or anyone (including ourselves) absolutely. Innocence means to become as a child and see every moment as new and interesting. Jesus said, "Unless you become as a little child you shall not enter the Kingdom of Heaven" (I believe what he meant by "Kingdom of Heaven" was enlightenment).

To experience innocence is to be freed from the constraints that our beliefs about reality impose upon the ever-fresh present. To experience innocence is to be empowered to see creative possibilities in every moment. To experience innocence is to know humility, to be aware of the extent of our limitations. To experience innocence is to be, comparatively, sane.

❖

Sixty years ago the development of thermonuclear weapons introduced the unprecedented possibility of human self-extinction. Now we've added the threat of self-extinction due to human-induced climate change. This unique state of affairs—no other species is known to have self-annihilated—is an indicator that humanity has neared a critical turning point.

The development of the capacity for abstract thought was the greatest evolutionary advance after the dawn of life. This is what marked human beings' fateful branching off from the wild animal kingdom. As the human brain increased in processing ability, the analytical/evaluation filter grew in complexity. Inevitably, subjective opinions would be confused with objective facts; everyone would suffer from delusional insanity. Individuals who were relatively sane would be rare and their contributions enormous.

Throughout history, human behavior has remained essentially unchanged. People worked, reproduced, fought wars, loved, and died with consequences that were overwhelmingly local. Civilizations rose and fell but human survival was never in doubt. This is no longer true.

The industrial revolution was the catalyst that sparked this change. Humans quickly began to reap tangible benefits from mass production and machines. In a comparative eye-blink of time (a few hundred years or so) extraordinary numbers of human beings have been liberated from the slavery of poverty and ignorance and the rule of queens, kings, and emperors.

As the machine age re-invented and refined itself into the information revolution the size of the educated population has grown exponentially. An unparalleled number of humans have gained three privileges heretofore restricted to a tiny elite: (a) comparative affluence, (b) education, and (c) the leisure time to contemplate the meaning of that education.

Now, thanks to science and technology, the three essential ingredients for a working philosopher—enough money to be educated and the resources to contemplate that education (as opposed to devoting every moment working to survive)—were available to unprecedented numbers. In short, the ground was laid for a critical mass of lay philosophers to begin to think critically.

In addition, the window to the world provided by mass media and the Internet has created an unprecedented bird's-eye view of our collective subjective-mind-dominated behavior.

The scientific/technological revolution was a blessing—and a curse. While the positive by-products of the industrial revolution and all that followed brought hope of liberation from the darkness of ignorance and poverty, we remain slaves to our subjective minds. Therefore the contributions of science and technology are far from being universally positive.

The same science and technology that gave us electric lights and refrigeration, miracle drugs and bypass surgery, freeways and flight, simultaneously gave us mass-produced machine guns, hydrogen bombs, chemical and biological weapons, and pollution. Chainsaws and bulldozers are currently doing immense damage to the forests of Earth, but they are not in and of themselves a problem. The problem comes from the confused minds that use them.

There is a race on, and the fate of humankind depends on the outcome. Will overpopulation, pollution, and environmental destruction alter the climate so dramatically that humans can no longer exist on this planet? Will accidental or intentional use of thermonuclear weapons destroy human civilization?

Or will enough people recognize that their perception of reality is a mind-generated delusion in time to change humanity's course?

This unprecedented situation—the human race standing in peril of destruction by its own hand—is the motivation for us to not only question our personal Story, but also our Cultural Story.

Because subjective mind is the principal source of our insanity and our self-hatred it is easy to regard it as an evil thing. This is incorrect. We must not demonize subjective mind because subjective-mind domination must logically be as perfect as everything else in the universe.

Subjective-mind domination is a state of confusion. Insanity is a state of confusion. Subjective-mind dominated behavior is an inevitable chapter in the evolutionary process: perfectly evolving apeoids perfectly trying to figure it all out making perfectly horrendous mistakes in the process. Perfect confusion. Perfect insanity.

I don't know what the future will bring, but I'm optimistic. From my point-of-view humans are an amazing, creative, and adaptive species. I think we'll make it.

One thing, however, is certain. Whatever the outcome, human self-extinction or human transcendence, it will be *perfect*.

About the Author

Kathleen Brugger is a philosopher, writer, videographer, and entrepreneur. Kathleen has a B.A. from Northwestern University in molecular biology and biochemistry. She is the co-author, with her husband Arthur Hancock, of *The Game of God: Recovering Your True Identity*. She lives in Asheville, North Carolina with Arthur and their cat, Kitty Cat.

Connect online at KathleenBrugger.com. For more insights about universal human insanity, visit the We Are ALL Innocent by Reason of Insanity website, www.InnocentByReasonofInsanity.com.

End Notes

Throughout the book, I have used "Webster's New Universal Unabridged Dictionary" as my source of definitions. http://www.merriam-websterunabridged.com/

1   *Mark Twain's Notebook*, Mark Twain, p. 345
        archive.org/details/MarkTwainsNotebook

2   Anthropologists' view of race:
        aaanet.org/stmts/racepp.htm
        The American Anthropological Association published a
        "Statement on 'Race'" in 1998; note the fact that the group
        put race in quotes. Their conclusion is that race is an invented
        concept, developed by European colonial powers to justify
        exploitation of the rest of the planet.

3   *The Heart is a Lonely Hunter*, Carson McCullers
        [Houghton Mifflin, 1940]

4   "Brain Time," by David Eagleman, 2009
        edge.org/conversation/brain-time

5   Triumph the Insult Comic Dog:
        youtu.be/LHa7iQJ_fEw

6   *Monty Python and the Holy Grail*, 1975 film
        youtube.com/watch?v=zIV4poUZAQo&list=UUGm3CO6LP
        cN-Y7HIuyE0Rew
        (at very beginning of clip can see servant with coconuts)

7   "The Boxer," Paul Simon, released 1969
        paulsimon.com/us/music/paul-simons-concert-park-august-
        15-1991/boxer

8   The Far Side, by Gary Larson, thefarside.com/

9   Discovery of galaxies:
         earthguide.ucsd.edu/virtualmuseum/ita/04_1.shtml

10   *Up From Eden*, Ken Wilber (New Science Library, 1981)
         p. 103-4
         Journey to Ixtlan, Carlos Castaneda (Simon and Schuster,
         1972)

11   Peter Paul Rubens, especially his "Venus" portraits
         peterpaulrubens.org/

12   Dutch tulip bubble:
         wikipedia.org/wiki/Tulip_mania
         In the 1630s a craze for tulips swept the Netherlands and the
         price of bulbs skyrocketed.
         A futures market in tulip bulbs was created, and farmers and
         workers sold everything they could to buy into the market. A
         single bulb was as valuable as a house. Then one day the
         market crashed—consensual reality had gotten too far out of
         touch with actual reality—and the price of a tulip bulb
         dropped to a more rational level.

13   "The Meaning of Life," Monty Python, (film) transcript:
         sfy.ru/?script=mp_meanlife

14   Roy Grinker study:
         ncbi.nlm.nih.gov/pmc/articles/PMC1575075/
         Dr. Grinker coined the term "homoclite" to describe a
         psychologically normal individual; he also did a follow-up
         study of the same individuals fourteen years later:
         archpsyc.jamanetwork.com/article.aspx?articleid=491142

15   *A Path with Heart*, Jack Kornfield
         (NY: Bantam Books, 1993), p. 23

16   *This Is It*, Alan Watts, [Colliers Book, 1967 paperback] p. 26
         (originally published 1958)

17   *A New Earth: Awakening to Your Life's Purpose*, by Eckhart Tolle [Penguin, 2005], paperback p. 73

18   "Song of Myself," *Leaves of Grass*, Walt Whitman

19   *Zen and the Art of Motorcycle Maintenance*, Robert Pirsig [William Morrow, 1974]

20   I won't pretend to have read *A Critique of Pure Reason*, by Immanuel Kant. This information is from general books on philosophy.

21   *Incognito: The Secret Lives of the Brain*, David Eagleman, [Pantheon Books, NY: 2011], p. 83

22   Abstract reasoning in animals: chimpanzees and apes, evidence also in parrots. See: blogs.smithsonianmag.com/science/2012/08/african-grey-parrots-have-the-reasoning-skills-of-3-year-olds/

23   *Pilgrim at Tinker Creek*, Annie Dillard, 1974

24   Pawan Sinha at TED conference, November 2009, "How Brains Learn to See" ted.com/talks/lang/eng/pawan_sinha_on_how_brains_learn_to_see.html

25   *The Mind's Eye*, Oliver Sacks [Alfred A. Knopf, 2010] p. 73 [originally read in "A Man of Letters," *The New Yorker*, June 28, 2010, page 22]

26   Beau Lotto TED Talk: ted.com/talks/beau_lotto_optical_illusions_show_how_we_see.html 3:20 – 4:35 (it's interesting from the beginning)

27   *The Fabric of Reality*, David Deutsch [Penguin, 1997] p. 120-1, 136

28   *The Invisible Gorilla: And Other Ways our Intuitions Deceive Us*, Christopher Chabris and Daniel Simons [Crown Publishers, 2010]

29   *Great Ideas in Physics*, Alan Lightman [McGraw-Hill, 2000]

30   Fads in science:
        From *Hidden Reality: Parallel Universes and the Deep Laws of the Cosmos*, by Brian Greene [Vintage, 2011], p, 230:
        "Hugh Everett, in his PhD thesis in 1956, suggested that the concept of multiverses could bridge the gap between Albert Einstein's and Neils Bohr's positions on probability. But this paper was ignored until Neils Bohr died because no one wanted to go against the orthodoxy of the day."

31   Rembrandt's self-portraits:
        rembrandtpainting.net/rembrandt_self_portraits.htm

32   Ch'ing Yuan, Eighth Century Buddhist Master
        See *Empty Logic: Madhyamika Buddhism from Chinese Sources*, by Hsueh-Li Cheng, p. 65-66

33   In about 200 AD Claudius Ptolemaeus developed a theory that explained planetary movements within a geocentric model of the universe that was accepted for 1500 years. Watch an animation of his theory here:
        britannica.com/EBchecked/media/13594/Ptolemys-theory-of-the-solar-system

34   *The Elephant Man*, David Lynch (1980 film)

35   Split-brain research: *The split brain: A tale of two halves*, by David Wolman, Nature, vol 483, Issue 7389, March 2012
        nature.com/news/the-split-brain-a-tale-of-two-halves-1.10213

36   *The User Illusion: Cutting Consciousness Down to Size*, by Tor Norretranders [Penguin, 1999] p. 283

37 *Thinking Fast and Slow*, Daniel Kahneman,
[Farrar, Straus and Giroux, 2011] p. 55, 128

38 *Incognito: The Secret Lives of the Brain*, David Eagleman,
[Vintage, 2012] p. 162

39 *The Power of Now: A Guide to Spiritual Enlightenment*,
by Eckhart Tolle [New World Library, 1999] p. 190

40 7-Up film series, Michael Apted, director;
wikipedia.org/wiki/Up_Series

41 Erik Erikson:
wikipedia.org/wiki/Erikson's_stages_of_psychosocial_develop
ment

42 Albert Einstein's Credo,
einstein-website.de/z_biography/credo.html
The passage in the Credo reads: "I do not believe in free will.
Schopenhauer's words: 'Man can do what he wants, but he
cannot will what he wills,' accompany me in all situations
throughout my life and reconcile me with the actions of
others, even if they are rather painful to me. This awareness
of the lack of free will keeps me from taking myself and my
fellow men too seriously as acting and deciding individuals,
and from losing my temper."

43 Einstein quote: *Physics and Philosophy*, by Sir James Jeans
[Dover, 1981], p. 213

44 *The User Illusion: Cutting Consciousness Down to Size*,
by Tor Norretranders [Penguin, 1999], p. 268

45 *Das Energi*, Paul Williams [Entwhistle Books, 1980]

46 *Thy Neighbor's Wife*, Gay Talese [Doubleday, 1980]

47 *Beyond Theology*, Alan Watts, [Vintage, 1973] p. 78
(originally published 1964)

48   *To Kill a Mockingbird*, Harper Lee
       [J.B. Lippincott and Co., 1960]

49   Carl Sagan quote:
       youtube.com/watch?v=MSce39QSYVo

50   *The Hitchhiker's Guide to the Galaxy*, Douglas Adams
       [Pan Books, 1979]

51   *Violence: Reflections on a National Epidemic*,
       by James Gilligan, MD [Grosset/Putnam Books, 1996] p. 11

52   *Talk of the Devil: Encounters With Seven Dictators*,
       by Riccardo Orizio [Walker and Co., 2004] p. 128

53   Dahmer condom use:
       nytimes.com/1992/02/16/us/milwaukee-jury-says-dahmer-
       was-sane.html?pagewanted=2

54   *Transforming the Mind: Teachings on Generating
       Compassion*, The Dalai Lama [Element Books, 2003]

55   John Hinckley verdict: *The Science of Good and Evil:
       Why People Cheat, Gossip, Care, Share, and Follow the
       Golden Rule*, Michael Shermer, [Times Books, 2004], p. 117

56   Tom Teepen:
       articles.chicagotribune.com/1991-05-24/news/
       9102160450_1_carl-hulsey-norman-sosebee-snowball
       Article quotes Teepen: "We are keener to understand and
       spare an abused goat than an abused human. Indeed, when a
       human kills, we sneer at his defense as a dodge— 'Yeah, yeah
       sure, his mother didn't love him'—yet we are sentimental
       about killer goats. We are a very strange animal."

57   *Care of the Soul*, by Thomas Moore
       [HarperCollins, 1992], p. 237

58   "Who's Afraid of Virginia Woolf?," by Edward Albee

59   *Zen and the Art of Motorcycle Maintenance,* Robert Pirsig
       [William Morrow, 1974]

60   Bob Dylan actually wrote: "Your debutante just knows what
       you need, but I know what you want," Song title: "Stuck
       Inside of Mobile with the Memphis Blues Again," Album:
       Blonde on Blonde

61   *The Wisdom of Insecurity,* by Alan Watts
       [Vintage edition 1968] p. 95 (willow), p. 117 (dance)
       (originally published 1951)

62   *Pleasantville,* 1998 film

63   Three Stooges, "Pardon My Scotch," 1935
       threestooges.net/

64   Socrates and oracle: *The Apology,* Plato
       classics.mit.edu/Plato/apology.html

65   *Laws of Form,* G. Spencer Brown (appendix 1); I've read in
       Center of the Cyclone: Looking Into Inner Space, by John C.
       Lilly [Ronin Publishing, Oakland CA, 1972], Introduction

66   Zen story (cup is full):
       101zenstories.com/index.php?story=1

67   *The Serial: A Year in the Life of Marin County,*
       by Cyra McFadden [Alfred A. Knopf, 1977], p. 27 (Ch. 10)

68   *Living Philosophies,* edited by Clifton Fadiman
       [Doubleday, 1990] p. 54

69   The Analects of Confucius, Book 2 Chapter 17
       gutenberg.org/cache/epub/3330/pg3330.html
       "The Master said, 'Yu, shall I teach you what knowledge is?
       When you know a thing, to hold that you know it; and when
       you do not know a thing, to allow that you do not know it;—
       this is knowledge.'"

70   Werner Erhard, wernererhard.com/est.html

71   "I'm the Duke University Freshman Porn Star,"
        xojane.com/sex/duke-university-freshman-porn-star

72   *Masters of Sex: The Life and Times of William Masters and
        Virginia Johnson, the Couple Who Taught America How to
        Love* Thomas Maier, [Basic Books, 2009], p. 181-2 hardback

73   Zen story (completion):
        goto.bilkent.edu.tr/gunes/ZEN/zenstories1.htm

74   Henry Ward Beecher; this quote is very commonly found
        in collections of quotations, but the original source is hard to
        find. One of the sermons in *The Sermons of Henry Ward
        Beecher in Plymouth Church, Brooklyn* (p. 23-26) expresses
        these same ideas (search google books).

75   *Stride Toward Freedom: The Montgomery Story,*
        by Martin Luther King, Jr. [Harper & Row, 1958]

76   *My Guru and His Disciple,* by Christopher Isherwood
        [Penguin, 1981]

77   Zorba the Greek (1964 film)

www.ingramcontent.com/pod-product-compliance
Lightning Source LLC
Chambersburg PA
CBHW070954040426
42443CB00007B/500